Fun Schway Interiors
North American Feng Shui

Mallory Neeve Wilkins
ASID IIDA IDC ARIDO

MDHD
Canada

Mallory Neeve Wilkins

Fun Schway Interiors
North American Feng Shui

Copyright August 2015 by Mallory Wilkins

All rights reserved. No part of this book may be used or reproduced by any means, graphic, electronic, or mechanical, including photocopying, recording, taping or by any information storage retrieval system without the written permission of the author/publisher.

The views expressed in this work are solely those of the author.

MDHD
Canada

ISBN: 978-0-9869035-3-3 ebook
ISBN: 978-0-9869035-4-0 paperback

Dedicated To
Mabelle
Joey
law

Contents

Introduction
One – Inspiration
Two – Surroundings
Three – Environmental Elements
Four – Awareness
Five – Relationships
Six – Knowledge
Seven – Attraction
Eight – Space Cleansing
Nine – Wisdom
Ten – Questions & Answers

Mallory Neeve Wilkins

INTRODUCTION

Ancient history, alchemy, science, philosophy and the mystical movement of energy are all part of the ongoing quest for a deeper understanding of life.

What happens when things go wrong, bad luck and mishaps keep coming your way? This means there is a lack of balance from deep within the ancient mystical flow of positive and negative energy within your environment. Loss and change will improve with corrections in your health, relationships, career, creativity and finances.

Today, television programs, books, webinars, CDs and other sources offer inspiration, self-help and creative solutions for an overall sense of well-being. *Feng Shui Interiors* will help you to understand and locate *your* positive energy by unfolding the the mystical movement of energy within and around you.

By taking a closer look at your home and environment, you will see that the way you treat them is a direct reflection of how others treat you. You need to understand how to change negative to positive energy within yourself, as well as in your environment. You may take yoga, tai ch'i, special medications or treatments, but if your environment isn't positive, then these other endeavors won't work to their potential.

Popular home improvement programs offer ways to enhance your lifestyle, home and surroundings with decorative designs and suggest *adding this, taking away that*, with healthier ways to live and suddenly you feel... Feng Shui energy. From many years of working in the design/build industry, planning, teaching, designing and working with energy, knowledgeable solutions are recommended for a healthier environment filled with prosperity and positive energy. It is *not* a science, philosophy or religion. It is a fact of life! The following theories and short stories offer numerous secret enhancements for the elements of everyday practice. These guidelines and questions & answers will improve your lifestyle, health, impact your mood and relationships - the North American way, through the ancient art of living in harmony with the environment. Good fun schway!

***

The Triangle Evolves

The GREAT ABSOLUTE *Formless Substance*
is an essence, which is undivided.
This *Silence* (static) produces *Formless Intelligence*,
the Creator, which is your inner *Intuition*.

Your thoughts create and your ideas become *Form*.
Another sees your *Form* (ideas)
From their *Formless Substance* (silence)
comes *Formless Intelligence* (creative-intuition)
and their thoughts and ideas become *Form*

Another sees their *Form*
- and -
The Triangle Evolves.

***

Good Fun Schway, says Grannie!

Why are you cleaning and painting Daddy's garage?
Because Daddy's work and finances are not doing well. His garage is very messy, so if we really clean it up and wash the car, we will watch and see if things get better for him. Because the garage is located in the Wealth area of this home, all his tools and garden things need to be placed in order so it looks cared for. We will change the negative energy to positive energy.

Why did you move the baby's crib?
Your baby sister has been twisting, turning and crying too much. She turns herself completely around in her crib. Her little body is automatically trying to move into her best energy field with her head facing north. We will make the changes and see her settle down, as this is the best direction for her to sleep for good Health.

Why are we taking our shoes off to walk in the grass?
It is a well-known fact that we all need to stay in contact with nature, feel the sun on our heads, feel the ground beneath our feet and feel the breath of the planet brush against our cheeks. We need to eat our fruits and vegetables. It is good to drink water that has sat in the sun for 3 hours because it has been enhanced with light. By doing this, we are nurturing our bodies.

Where did you get all those old books, Grannie?
Not so long ago in the 1970s, in a country called China, there was a rebellion against their ancient heritage traditions and a book called the "I Ching". The young people thought if they got rid of such beliefs they would be more accepted by modern day cultures, so they destroyed most of their ancient treasures and writings. Some books were taken to England, Japan, and San Francisco. These are my collections of the ancient Feng Shui teachings.

(One)
INSPIRATION

How is it that we receive ideas from out of nowhere without formal training?

Where does intuition come from?

Mystical Energy
Everything is alive connected and changing. As time passes, you will notice that your feelings toward different colors, shapes and elements will alter from year to year because of the earth's electromagnetic fields. Take note!

Feng Shui (energy movement of wind & water)
was once called '*Kan Yu*' meaning... cover & support, reflecting *Above & Below* or *Heaven & Earth* concepts, which were from the **"I Ching"** Book of Changes first collaborated nearly five thousand years ago.

Feng Shui knowledge
is from the ancient compass school study or classic teaching with a 5000-year-old history while new studies like 'Black Hat Sect' (Tibetan/Buddhist) was created in the USA in 1984 not conforming with the full concepts of the ancient sacred teachings.

The way you treat your home is a direct reflection of the way you are treated by others.

Free flowing energy is a 'river stocked with gifts". Learn to see, and have an eye for details. Remove blockages.

Energy is the breath of the planet. It is the 'momentum of life', which circulates through *everything.* Cleanse your environment by removing all damaged, cracked or broken things.

Universal Law
is said to be an 'interwoven life energy' made up of both 'good luck yang' and 'bad luck yin' ever creating the ups and downs. Write a

list of your life's path of ups and downs.

Yin/Yang
is the theory of opposites. The *Yin* side of the building would *not* be as bright as the *Yang* side. Where are you most comfortable?

Yin/Yang colors
Yin would be the dark side... (On a scale of 1–10 with 10 being black). Yin = 6 to 10 and Yang color spectrum would be from 1 to 5 on the lighter side.

Concept to Consider (The space)
There are many ways to understand the mystical movement of energy. Imagine a cube. Imagine a very large cube and let's call it... your bedroom and it contains 100% energy. There are two windows (fire-energy) and an entry door. If you place a bed into this space, and add pillows, bedding, mattress and side tables, then the energy within this space has been replaced, diminished or removed and is reduced to say, 80%. If you add artwork, tables, dresser and a chair then it is reduced further down to 55%. If you add TV, computer, desk, fill the closet with shoes, clothes and other items... pretty soon the flow of positive energy that should be reaching you.. has been reduced to 40% or less. The more stuff within a space means that you are receiving less and less and the positive energy can become negative, especially if the items are damaged, cracked, dirty or broken.

Personalized Energy
Everyone carries the energy of their *Birth Year* throughout their whole life. The energy of the year you were born affects your moods, likes and dislikes, friendships, creativity and health. An example would be... the year 1980 carries the energy of a "yang metal-energy year." Other specifications found on a 1980 energy chart for a female born in this year would be: her Pa kua is #4. She carries energy of an *East* person with positive energy locations of *north, east, south* and *southeast*; and the zodiac animal *Monkey* with positive energy numbers of 9, 4, 3 and 1. (Information is different if she was born very early in the year before the Chinese New Year changes. The readings are different for a male).

Enhance your aura and positive energy with a smile, whenever.

Luck and good fortune are founded on politeness, charity, and giving kindness whenever possible.

Feng Shui is the use of Natural Products.

Energy flow and it's movement is affected by weather, temperature, wind, storms, rain, snow and is also transmitted through media sounds, light and heat. Take note of your environment and its changes.

***

Thank your Lucky Stars!

Good luck and good fortune are cosmic stardusts that dance around the environment in an invisible state. That is what I learned many years ago.

A dog hears sounds that we don't hear. Many animals see things we don't see. In another dimension, there is a deeper awareness. Music can reach a pitch that goes unnoticed by humans, yet many other creatures can hear it.

Daydreaming can pass time, as we drive from one place to another without any recollection of the actual drive. There are many mysteries.

How is it that a tree of over one hundred feet in height developed from a minute seed is overwhelming to think about. Where does such power come from and why does it not just fall over?

The energy within us all is the same energy that boosts, and opens those seeds into mighty forests. How? Nature provides it from within the earth. (Yin Energy) At a particular temperature (fire energy), with just the right moisture (water energy), a current develops, and bingo! The breath, the wind, the power develops and from a dead looking tree of winter, blossoms millions of buds into leaves. Alchemy. Human beings would be Yang while the planet earth is Yin, and if humans can incorporate this Yin energy, possibilities can be endless.

This inner Earth energy is what makes us grow, developing

wisdom. Within our quiet times in a 'nature' setting, we can feel or hear it. Our intuition from the Great Absolute comes forth, nurturing our growth. Relax, walk in the country, in the quiet and listen. 'Stare' deeply at nature, focus onto something that appeals to your senses, and a new light within comes to you.

One of my enjoyments in life is teaching. I remember one special afternoon class, to a group of parents, was marked on my studio calendar. I arrived at the school and greeted by several grade two students. They informed me that I would be talking to their Moms and Dads in their classroom. A couple of them wanted to know if it would be o.k. if they could help me. They led the way as I followed them through the halls to the second floor classroom of the old brick building.

As we entered their classroom, Josh introduced himself and his friend Aaron. I opened my portfolio and withdrew my magic markers, in many colors. They liked that. A large flow chart was at the front of the classroom.

'What are you going to do first?' Josh asked as I began to draw a large circle.

Another student in a white eyelet, cotton dress approached with curious eyes. She announced herself as Betty but her name was Elizabeth Niziol. Her silky skin was a soft, milk chocolate color with a set of incredible large hazel eyes that sparkled with enthusiasm.

"What's that you are drawing?" Betty asked.

"Humm, what does it look like to you?" I replied with a smile.

"The moon" she responded. I continued with the Yin-Yang symbol, by separating the circle into two sections.

"No!" Josh shouted. "It's the earth, right?"

"What's that 'S' letter for in the middle of your circle?" asked Aaron impatiently. I continued by producing the Yin - Yang symbol, coloring one side dark, on the left, leaving a small open circle white in the middle, then placing the same small circle on the right white side and coloring it black.

"Oh... it's the earth, full of black and white people, right?" announced Josh. "It looks like a little bit of each mixed together, right?"

"Well, kids, it is actually a drawing indicating the balance of dark and light. You know about opposites? There is good and bad or perhaps hot and cold, up and down... so this indicates that the earth is in harmony. You can see that there is a little dark in the light section and a little white circle on the dark side." I paused.

"You mean there is a little good in the bad, and a little bad in the good." Josh pointed out excitedly.

"What do you think, Betty?" I asked, smiling.

"I see more dark than light. Maybe there is more bad than good. Maybe the 'S' shape is for Secret?"

You never know what comes out of the mouths of kids!

I showed them several black sheets of paper and asked them to place one on each desk. With a little pushing, they accomplished the task.

"What's this for?" asked Aaron.

"I am going to show your parents how to see their aura."

None of the children spoke, but each had an inquisitive eye, waiting for me to say something. Several minutes passed before Josh asked for the 'o-raw' to be explained.

"You and me, and everybody else are full of energy," I said looking and pointing at each one individually.

"I know," Aaron jumped in. "My Grandpa tells me that all the time. He tells me I have too much energy." I couldn't help but laugh.

"Well, your energy can be seen all around you as a soft shimmer or glow." The children's eyes widened, as I was going to produce magic for them. "Here, take a black piece of paper, and put it on the desk." The three of them quickly scrambled to find a place to sit near me, and got themselves ready for the next step.

I held both hands up shaking my fingers loosely. They instinctively copied my gestures before I asked them to do the same.

"This will activate your energy. Now, raise your two 'pointing' fingers, next to your thumbs... that's good." I showed them how to point the fingers together, fingernail to fingernail, inches above the piece of black paper, so that they would look at the inside of their hand with the index fingers pointing, and the other fingers curled in, towards their palm, with their thumbs pointing upwards.

"Now, don't let the two fingers touch. There must be a small space between them." The children had it down pat. I helped them align their hands just so. I told them they needed to stare down through the opening between the two pointing fingers, onto the black paper for a moment without blinking their eyes. Then, I asked them to slowly pull the hands apart from each other making the opening larger, and they would notice a shadow left from where their fingers had been, lingering over the black paper.

"Did you see that stream of mist?" The children nodded, and started chatting amongst themselves about this 'trick'. "Well, that mist is your personal 'aura'. Sometimes it may be a colored mist. And sometimes, when you are very relaxed and calm, staring at a person, you may see this shimmer of light all around their head or body. What you are actually seeing... is the 'energy' of that person.

"Can I see my own body energy?" asked 7-year-old Josh.

"Sure," I responded, "but you will have to relax and stare at yourself in the mirror." The children played with this idea for several minutes and pretended to see each other's energy.

"This is so much fun," exclaimed Betty.

"Do you know some more stuff?" Josh inquired jumping to his feet.

I finished drawing the outline of an eight-sided compass on the flip chart, setting my marker on the ledge nearby.

"Would you like to *feel* your energy?" They rambunctiously scattered around. I couldn't help but laugh at their enthusiasm. "OK... settle down. It won't work if you get all excited." They stood remarkably still. "You must be calm and focus."

I began rubbing my hands together, and before I could explain anything, they began mimicking my actions. I asked them to glance away or close their eyes. After fifteen seconds or so, I told them to release and separate their hands about four to six inches apart, letting the fingers relax, as if they were holding a ball and then move their hands back and forth ever so slightly, without touching.

"You will feel an invisible cushion, like a cotton ball. A soft pressure you feel is your energy that you have activated. You are now feeling the shadow you saw on the black piece of paper, that stream of mist."

"Cool!" exclaimed Aaron.

"Remember kids. When you are happy, full of joy and love, you have a big, bright energy field. When you are sad, hurt or hateful, you have small, dark energy. So be full of fun and laughter, and you will attract good fortune."

At that moment, their parents arrived and entered the classroom to hear me speak about the 'Mystical movement of Energy'. I allowed the young students to begin the program with their demonstrations and drawing of the Yin-Yang symbol. Their amazing efforts were a big hit. When it came time to sit, they tip-toed to the back of the room and waited patiently during my hour talk, never making a sound, eager to learn.

Good fun schway... says Grannie!

***

Be aware of things, places, and people that offend or are a bother. Identify them by recording the information,

Poison Arrows
are referred to as sharp pointed edges pointing in our direction... such as the 'corner edge' of wall; a file cabinet corner; furniture with straight sharp edges; overhead beams, satellite dishes, etc.

A known fact is that Feng Shui energy travels in a curve. It is meandering. Identify straight-line paths in your environment, as this is identified as a poison arrow, referring to a direct attack, which threatens to wound.

The mystical movement of energy is an 'awareness' art.
When making any 'corrections' to your environment, it should be recorded (in a journal) and written with your intent for improvement.

Feng Shui advises: too large or too many windows = vulnerability for the occupants.

The ancient masters cautioned that no one should sit with their back to an entry door of a room, especially when sitting at a table eating. If there is no alternative, place a mirror nearby so you always are in control of who/what is behind you.

Missing areas:
When something is missing from your life... look closely at the shape and floor plan (design) of your building and see where there is lack, or missing areas, which need restoring, fixing or cleansing.

Correct energy movement is created by setting up rooms so that no chair or sofa has its back to any doorway, preventing or blocking the calming flow of energy to enter.

Space planning and proper placements need complete organization, as open shelves are negative with their cutting edge shelves. Display items (mixed) into groupings so energy can move throughout the space; never overcrowd shelves.

Furniture: Sofas, couches and chesterfields should *not* be stacked with pillows – closing all opportunities for 'new' to enter. Be ready for new things, ideas and openings by keeping one side clear, not blocking up any new opportunities.

Art Placement is recommended 2-3" apart when collaborating items into groupings on a wall.

Lighting: ceiling fixtures like chandeliers require a thirty-inch space above an eating table when in a space with eight-foot high walls or thirty-six inch in a room with nine-foot walls.

Interior flow is best when 'round' edge furniture is used, which is more conducive to smooth flowing energy.

Feng Shui dictates balance and an adequate distance between conversational seating, which is an eight-foot distance for easy energy movement.

Negative energy cleanses:
A cleanse is needed for protection from waste products, dirty clothes, etc. These kinds of things should always be covered or located under tables or behind a closet door to help control the damaging flow within a sleeping or work space for personal clarity.

Stagnant energy: created and found when an 'item' that is not touched, used or loved turns negative and spreads its energy throughout the space. Take a walk through each room... having an eye for detail... once a month and remove such 'unused' items - a collectable that is no longer admired or appreciated.

***

Sports Trauma

Spring time is when we are suppose to throw open our windows, move the furniture, scrub down, toss out and get rid of old baggage. It wasn't until June that I finally got my act together to undertake this yearly task.

A freshness arrived with the morning breeze as I began working on the bedroom closets. I had three large garbage bags set to one side. One marked... 'throw-away', another marked 'keep-items' and a third, 'not-sure'. The third bag was for items that were 'maybes' but not allowed back into the closet if not loved, needed or used regularly. The idea? If items were left untouched or not used within the past five months, they were no longer needed, and if they were loved, they would have been used, so to speak.

Whenever you 'space cleanse' an area using Feng Shui techniques, it is recommended to collect the five natural elements together and play your favorite music while working. I use an old silver tray (metal) where I place a wooden candleholder (wood), with a red candle (fire), and small amount of ocean water in a clear glass container (water) next to a quartz crystal (earth). You can purchase kits already put together, but I recommend that you consider the five elements and make up your own personal one from items you may already own. This helps in clearing out old energies; like after a nasty quarrel, burnt dinner, or unwanted visitor. The concept of an 'Energy clearing' kit is for you to activate the five elements as you clean out the negative energy. Play the music, light the candle; pour out some water, etc.

During this particular exercise, I walked by my son's room (the athlete) while fetching the vacuum and casually looked in, noticing the long empty wall across from the entry door. I commented that he needed something interesting to hang on it, as there wasn't even a window. I continued with what I was doing.

Whenever you are making a change or cleansing, it is important to do it yourself as your personal energy provides maximum effect.

Within a few hours, my empty closet had been washed down, vacuumed and any disrepairs were fixed. My choice of Cat Stevens music might not have appealed to my teenagers, but it did the trick for me. I used matching red coat hangers (because my birth year energy is Yin Fire) and discarded all others. I left 10% of the hangers empty to show I was always ready for 'new' to come into my life. I figured that I could use some prosperity and good luck, so I decided to leave 15% empty instead.

The *closet* is usually the first and last space we use during the day. Whether before bed or first thing in the morning, we want to make sure we attract positive energy to begin or end our day. You will find it refreshing to feel a sense of calmness once it is organized.

- Arrange all clothes into color groups, not by items. I placed everything white/beige tones all together; another section had dark tones of black/browns etc. These color groups should *not* be mixed to appear orderly.
- Nothing on the floor unless contained in a box, basket or (floor) mat.
- If something's *not* used within the last five months, get rid of it. It should not be there becoming stagnant when not being used, or touched. Stagnant energy is negative.
- A most important note; never overcrowd or jam a space. This can bring about a cluttered mind and memory loss.

When I had completed all the upper level closets, I gathered my four bags (amazing how things accumulate) of 'stuff' to get rid of, and passed by the bedroom of my son, the cyclist-surfer athlete, noticing that he had placed a couple of his competitive cycling shirts on the wall behind the head of his bed. This is not a good idea, and I intended to mention this to him. The head of the bed must be kept clear at all times, for the meandering positive energy to reach you during sleep. Because it had been a busy time of year for cyclists as competitions had begun, he was heading to Whistler for a *Trials* event. (This extreme sport had become very popular on the west coast.)

The following week, all my bags of worldly collections were distributed to either Big Brother or Women In Need organizations. Remember – it is best to give away anything you can, and then the old is renewed, as a gift in kind. Sell items on EBay or Craigslist and donate the proceeds to your favorite charity.

Another day passed when my daughter brought up the fact that her brother had something over the head of his bed. 'Did I not know he had displayed two of his cycling shirts?" I had neglected to mention this. Again, it's important to note that nothing should be around the head of the bed for clarity, and a good night sleep, so that the energy is not distracted by 'items' near or under the bed. It was later that very evening that we got a phone call from the hospital. He was in Emergency getting stitches from a bike mishap.

Trials is definitely an extreme sport of obstacle riding, climbing, jumping and trick performing that often can cause accidents if the rider is not totally focused. This time, his scraped arms, bloody nose, scared legs were topped-off with stitches to the chin. Of course, it is never bad enough to rethink the sport. It just adds to the challenge, so I was told.

We joked that he should know better than to attract negative energy to his sport and to himself by doing such a thing.

After a few days of rest and a lecture from his sister, his shirts were removed from over his bed. It's not that it didn't look pretty cool, but with all the Feng Shui techniques around our home, he should have known better. She took one look at his wall, pointed the finger at the shirts, and shook her head. He got the hint.

Warning: remove anything from over or under the bed, and keep the energy calm and clear around your head when sleeping. It's a health issue. We must make sure that the incoming positive energy is not distracted, so that our sleep is peaceful. This clarity can help keep our memory sharp. Reflective surfaces are the worst. No mirrors allowed. When the energy hits the item, it can turn negative before it reaches the one asleep... thereby the negative energy influenced a cycling accident, perhaps.

The bedroom needs to be free from clutter for good health and prosperity with nothing lying around on the floor, which helps keep relationships strong. We spend the majority of our hours in this room, where other rooms we tend to spend only a short time in each.

Another day and we looked at the athlete's bedroom. A handsome poster of himself performing Trials hung several feet away from his bed over his desk on the same long wall, which was a much better idea. It solved the problem of an empty wall and now gave him an identity in his favorite sport, or was it surfing?

Good fun schway... says Grannie!

***

NOTES:

Feng Shui is a balance of yin/yang so that every space should represent 'calm' with no clutter and all things 'contained' (pots/baskets/trays etc) for maximum abundance and a sense of well being.

Body-balance energy is an organic system. The *I Ching* (Book of Changes) 5000 years ago began explaining that there are as many internal changes as there are environmental changes.

Feng Shui warns about using octagon shapes in the interior of buildings, which can cause havoc.

Electronics are 'metal' elements and operate best in the west area of a room, especially when placed next to something round to enhance positive energy.

Straight lines cause positive energy to change to negative energy because it flows too quickly down corridors, hallways, etc. Energy paths should meander gently.

Just as life evolves, the art of placement is important. 'Changes' in residence, color, apparel, etc. are required for needed corrections as *routine* causes stagnant energy. (It's not any different than the relocation of ancient tribes from place to place... or, the seasonal changes in nature, and the changing trends in fashion.)

Every space carries different energy.
A boardroom function differs from a spa, or a kitchen differs from a bedroom. Be conscious of these differences and how you feel in each space when you enter. Some rooms you are attracted into, while others, you never want to enter.

Feng Shui energy change or correction is accomplished through color, shapes or an element item (fire = lamp) which can actually introduce significant changes.

'Peaches' in still-life art and *deer* in landscape artwork enhance longevity in ancient days; pine & bamboo were used in landscape gardens as well as the chrysanthemums.

Natural items such as light, sound, music can enhance and

encourage positive energy to any aspiration/sector of a building when 'just the right level' is found.

Remedies: natural elements are preferred in healthy environments. Replace all dried (past 6 months) and plastic flowers with silk or growing plants.

Everything is made up of energy.
Wash your car regularly and notice how it seems to run and look better.

Objects that stimulate energy are (a) shiny surface objects (b) flags (c) color

Art: Family photos belong in the southwest sector of a room for Relationship enhancement and improvement. Hallways and corridors are another good space for them to hang.

Relationships: Truthful communication is the way to improve relationships. Speak your truth only when facing your best direction (from you Pa Kua chart) for positive results.

Energy flow into a room from the front entry door flows straight ahead, deflecting back off the wall across the room. It is never wise to sit in its path (incoming energy) until it slows down so not to encourage anxiety or headaches.

Zen Rooms are calm spaces without electronics and high-energy colors, but they should contain the five natural elements for harmony and balance.

Mirrors should be removed from places of business unless retail. This specific item needs to be considered carefully.

Electronic clutter is a combination of excessive wires, cords, plugs and must be contained & hidden from incoming energy flow so not to weaken it.

Change is good.
Activate energy by moving accessories regularly; changing the art, pillows, table top decor, mantle displays, wall groupings etc.

Less is Best: If you don't love something or use it - get rid of it - or the incoming energy will only enhance something you don't want. It is like hanging onto old baggage that just won't go away.

Smooth Going: Things in your life flow smoothly when you situate yourself in your Personal Best space. Know and remember your four best locations for positive energy. This is dictated from the Pa-Kua calculations using your birth year.

Your home is a reflection of who you are and your inner personality. Look around. Remove all energy blocks.

Personal items, such as your interest in books or magazines, can be visible on shelves, in baskets or stacked to raise a low lamp for better reading, but not scattered.

Be mindful of your personal space and aware of its energy. By making just one alteration to your space, watch for feedback into your life (journal it) before you introduce another correction.

Beware of dark buildings.
Different environments suit different types of people. Realtors know this better than most that closed houses are Yin energy (dark) and everyone that enters brings in Yang (from the outside) energy along with their own energy pattern, either positive or negative. Cleanse the space with candles if you have a bad reaction after visitors have departed your home.

Continuity brings harmony. Balance a rooms color, furniture placement, five natural elements with upper and lower items such as crown moldings (high) carpets (low).

Reflective surfaces magnify the energy flow. Framed pictures and mirrors are well placed in spaces like a dining room, but not in a bedroom; each having a different effect on the occupants health.

Beauty: A single item of beauty can attract more abundance and correction into your life than having many items. Less is best.

Connection to past: Remove items that hold connection to past difficulties. Light candles while making new adjustments. No 'past baggage' aloud while focusing on new, prosperous ventures, relationships or creativities. This can be true if you have inherited furniture that came into your home from 'not a happy place or relationship.'

Keep yourself positive by preparing your clothes the night before. This starts the energy flow and 'control', as the selection or decision was created before rising.

Dark 'yin' days: are brightened by wearing the color yellow 'somewhere'. Add yellow flowers to a room. Always listen or watch comedies, which are all good remedies for the 'blues'.

Keep yourself positive by identifying deep-rooted problems by writing or speaking to another person. Problems must be released from within to cleanse the clutter from the body so sickness and pain are removed.

Cleaning the outer environment is just half of the problem correction. Clean up your inner self (This harmonizes yin/yang energies) after you have done your environment because the outside energy affects your inner energy healing abilities.

Not coping well with life's changes can be from too much black (water element) as one seeks the dark; winter. Add touches of red (fire) or white (metal) to the space or your wardrobe where the dark dominates.

Identify your space with items that stimulate you, and remove everything that doesn't. What you loved yesterday, you may dislike today. Your life will flow much smoother and surprisingly new things come to you.

If you need change in your life, give away something that you really love or need creating a void, so unexpected happenings have room to enter your life. *Gifts given away; many gifts received.*

(Two)
SURROUNDINGS

On a warm spring April day, one morn
A little bitty seed of a tree was born, in the garden.
With all the warmth of the land it grew
Loved by the rain and the soft warm dew, in the garden.
As it reached for the sky, from a power within,
It's soul cried out and its beauty began.
Love came through from the earth below
And it's energy was the power to grow, in the garden.
Just look around, and you will see
All the love coming from this tall green tree,
in the garden.

Every morning, as you begin your day
First, look at nature that shows you the way,
Does it look grand, strong and bold?
This means your way will be the path of gold.
If the wind and water and plants seem down,
Don't make plans or decisions right now.
It's nature's way of reflecting your day,
So keep this in mind, it's our secret, we say.

***

Feng Shui is an example of practical ancient art, which can secure prosperity, respect, good fortune and creativity. Therefore, let it be known that the entrance to any building should be in clear view; a vision of beauty to encourage good, positive energy to enter.

Ch'i energy must reflect your personal taste, as the design layout of your building is your energy path, which the ancient masters mapped from the mysterious earth forces. Therefore, your environment affects you.

Pay attention to your intuition, the perfect balance of Yin/Yang – which is the small voice that speaks to you from within, known as *Formless Intelligence*.

Yin/Yang forces run through the earth. Your bodies (chakra) and your buildings must be acknowledged and kept in balance so not to be damaged or weakened.

Birth year Energy: According to your birth year, you are identified as an *East* or *West* person. The most prosperous building for an *east* person is one that the entry door faces *north* or *south*.

A *West* person's prosperous building is one that the entry door faces *southwest* or *northeast*.

Moving or relocating: Apply Feng Shui principals to buildings you are moving into, so you know the energy will be healthy and suitable to all and not a place where nagging, arguing and harassment takes place.

Learn about the *history of a house* before you move in, and its facing direction and location (where it "sits") as well as why the people before you moved out of the property. Houses have karma and tend to repeat their histories. Buyer beware.

Structure: A building carries certain energy from ALL those who built it, lived in it as well as visited. Your intuition is a perfect balance of Yin/Yang energy and tells you if it is right for you. Listen, always, to your Inner Voice.

Exterior improvements: Increase the supply of beneficial energies that flow into the building. Your exterior environment and surroundings represent your past, present and future (in metaphysical terms). Strong 'rear' support (hill) represents the past and should not be overshadowed on the sides. Have an open clear front view, future with the front being open without obstruction; clear path with no obstacles.

Beautiful views are highly nurturing to the building's occupants. (windows; art; photography)

Warning to the owner, to act wisely and know if there were any financial difficulties with the previous owners, so not to carry 'vertically' these misfortunes, hardships.

Exterior knowledge is to make an effort to know all you can about the history of the lot & building & its previous occupants for any unhappy or damaging incidents.

Overhead wires should be situated away from the front of the building so not to over activate the 'Metal' elements of the building – damaging to one's health.

Observe exterior locations. Don't be overshadowed by a neighboring large building, as it absorbs the 'good fortune' energy away from you.

Entrance Path lighted to the entry door attracts positive flowing energy just as flowers do in the daytime.

Identify the building's address numbers, as these must be placed on the **vertical** OR **horizontal;** if not, this is a sign of indecisiveness when placed on an angle,

Building numbers must be visible from the road or else the incoming energy knows you are hiding something from others. A sense of clarity is reflective of your personality.

Overgrown landscaping prevents new opportunities from entering your life as the structure disappears behind neglected gardens diminishing the energy flow.

Exterior landscaping such as shrubs blocking the entry should be removed so prosperous energy enters the building without blockage that can change the flow to negative.

Remove landscaping and overgrown gardens that block the *view* of any window and prevents the 'sun' (fire element) from entering the building, which enhances the owners 'abundance' and 'health', which could be diminished, suddenly.

Exterior clearing is accomplished by removing any obstruction blocking the view or entry path to the main entrance of the building.

Walkways should be kept in good order, without weeds, cracks or damage so not to bring negative & 'loss' energy into the building.

Landscaping: be cautious about the placement of 'spiky' plants and shrubs, which can damage/change the flow of energy to negative if they are *not* situated next to 'round' leave greenery for balance.

Curb appeal can be weakened or damaged by viewing broken fences, gates, steps, weeds, clutter and neglect, showing apparent weakening of the *abundance* energy around the building.

Caution of 'sharp' protruding corners when entering a building. They should be 'softened' with plants, as these corners represent 'poison arrows'. They take the shape (pointed edge) of an arrowhead tip. These cutting edges reflect 'bruising of the energy as it passes'.

Exterior beauty diminishes just like your good fortune, when the windows are dirty or chipped paint is apparent.

Sidewalks and garden edges: keep them manicured and trimmed, free of weeds so that neglect doesn't attract negative energies that could bring sickness into the building.

Always repair *any* broken, damaged or cracked areas to keep illness away. Damaged areas weaken the Creativity-energy of the occupants.

Exterior drains, eaves troughs must be free from clutter so the water and debris flow freely making sure that the energy around the environment flows freely, and stays positive.

Exterior 'entry' doors; identify separately by painting only the front door an accent color to enhance its location and attract positive energy. Color selection follows the direction (choices) in which it faces. (south-red tones; east-green tones etc). This colour is not used elsewhere on the exterior of the house.

Front Door hardware should operate smoothly without stiffness, or damage and work easily to make sure any 'hardships' stay out of the building.

Entry sound systems (intercoms, doorbells etc) should be repaired if broken or not operating correctly so not to encourage mishaps/accidents, as any damaged, broken or cracked items can!

Obstructions needs to be noted, such as lampposts, trees or any objects directly in front of the entry, as these vertical items can 'cut the energy' and weaken it upon entering the building, thereby preventing new friendships.

Nothing should touch, interfere or hinder the structure, especially the roof, so not to add anxiety to the occupants.

Buildings with no yard/property, or that have a steep drop, leaves the occupants with 'no backing' and possibly financially poor. Buildings prosper with the mountain or high building' behind them for support.

Health enhancement by collecting rainwater in glass containers (earth element) supports the water element by enhancing its energy. Collect the rainwater and let it sit 3 hours outside in the sun. This actually helps one's memory when taken regularly and can enhance plant life.

Walkways: beware of straight lines!
Walkways to the entry of the building where energy enters can become destructive and move too fast. <u>Curved entries</u> are recommended to keep the energy prosperous.

Exterior corners can become 'traps' if left empty and the energy becomes stagnant. Place an attractive item or greenery there for protection.

Undulating mystical movement of energy can be achieved with flags located strategically on the property.

Outside Chimes should be conducive to its location as 'metal' chimes in the west will bring good fortune, while 'wood' chimes only in the east and 'crystal' in the southwest or northeast so not to bring harm to the building or occupants.

The Location of your building is best situated on the 'inside' of a curved road rather than on the 'outside' bend of the curved road for its protection.

Exterior location of a building where a roadway directed right at it becomes overpowered by swift moving energy reducing all sense of calmness.

Enhancement: created by a wide-open space around the front entry enhanced by 'life' elements (greenery).

Supportive energy: achieved when a high building or hill is located behind your building.

Remember: Energy is powerful – just because we cannot see its flow, you can definitely feel its presence. (Wind is the breath of the planet).

***

Environmental Issues

Following a Conference in New York City and a House Tour at Street of Dreams in Seattle, it was plain to see that the Architects of the day were finally aware of the health issues of their buildings. Synthetics and off-gassing products they created were causing havoc and needed to be brought to the public's attention. This movement didn't take place until the late nineties, even though most designers knew the problems during the eighties as doctors offices were full of patients complaining of headaches, sore muscles, asthma, slow loss of memory, etc.

We start our day with plastic toothbrushes and eat food from plastic packaging. We wear clothes containing more man-made fibers than natural fibers. We look through plastic lenses in our glasses and drive plastic vehicles. Will it never end? Petroleum products have created this Plastic Planet, and it is killing us with poor health and disease. You wonder why we are not healthy!

Alternative natural products are needed throughout our home. Let's be aware and read labels, and make healthier choices. These chemical based products are stagnant energy and prevent the positive flow from entering. It's about keeping our children and planet in good health. These sickly chemically enhanced products are now showing up in our DNA.

Condo living created another worry for the homeowner who has no choice when selecting a lot of the interior finishes. The developers and suppliers have come up with solutions so that wood floorings can now be installed, but the majority of it is constructed from a composite with glue-based chemically enhanced fibers. Tile flooring can now replace vinyls, laminate floorings and chemically enhanced carpets. We need more wool, hemp, cotton products and wood that lasts, which are durable and healthier for us all.

When you enter a building, whether at work or at home, you can feel the difference when there are no open windows to cleanse the air. Groups of students living in an enclosed area often complain of sore muscles, throats and headaches. Elderly people become ill only months after relocating into a 'newer' residence when they use to live in an older home for years. These new facilities are put together in the shortest time possible and carry the cheapest made products a lot of the time. The negative energy created by the off-gassing is harmful. Add plants to the space to help cleanse the air.

In Portland, Oregon, Elizabeth Olsen inherited some beautiful pieces of furniture from relatives, and placed the wool oriental carpets over the already existing synthetic carpets reducing the effect to a minimum. The real wood furniture and natural content fabrics in the furniture were what our parents grew up with, and they were a lot healthier then, than now. They weren't exposed to fiberboard construction used in today's products or the formaldehyde. Wood was real wood, not filled with 'other' things, non-biodegradable chemical products and excessive resins.

When Elizabeth was updating her home, she worried when neighbors found mould during a renovation. She was lucky and found none. She selected a water based stain for her new maple bathroom vanity, granite counter top and beautiful tiles for her shower surround and heated floor. Her new floor was limestone and the walls constructed out of concrete board instead of drywall before tiling. Removing all the plastic hardware, replacing it with brushed nickel, there was no more vinyl so she could actually breathe better and felt more energetic.

Feng Shui is about the *feeling* and balancing the energies. When the energy can flow and meander throughout the space, it is positive. You will actually feel happier.

Most of us like to work or live in new accommodations, but after a few months you tend to feel tired a lot more than usual. You may suffer anxiety, headaches or stiffness. These are the interior problems of sick-building syndrome, SBS.

Exterior Environment is your curb appeal, which is an investment that can increase the value of your home, just by enhancing the structure with the right colors. Your home is the largest single investment made by 94% of North Americans.

Many older homes in Port Hope, Ontario are beautifully displayed with color. Vicki Irwin owned a home in this neighborhood, and was reluctant to select colors. The front entry faced west, (metal-energy) so a heritage Cashmere Gray color was chosen. The color on the front door should *not be used* elsewhere on the structure so that the unseen energy has no difficulty flowing in the right direction, and this strong statement lets everyone else know as well. This smaller home sat next to a much larger one, so her exterior design needed to be invigorating. The field was a rich charcoal shade; the windows were White Sand with terra cotta colored shutters. The roof trim and fascia boards had terra cotta edges. Gutters and eaves blended into the color of the roof, whenever possible. The garage door(s) color is the same as the field of the house, so not to attract energy to a negative place of tools, garbage bins, etc.

Color can make a strong statement and is a carrier of energy. It not only has to look good, it has to feel good. Exterior color should not be fashionable or too trendy, so not to appear dated in a few years. Your colors should complement the architecture, structure with its placement.

Terra cotta planters complemented Vicki's entry and were all filled with one color of flowering plants, but in different varieties. She was pleased, saying the house even felt happier, all because of the energy change.

A Feng Shui house is under the influence of the elements. The wind and the rain will change the exterior and its colors will fade. Cracks, breaks and damage to the structure will appear; plants and shrubs overgrow their space, as more cracks appear in the walkways, etc. The changing energy from the elements, affected by the movement and vibrations of the planets, is no different from our bodies and personalities that are ever changing. Beware of the forces of nature. To keep all things in harmony, one must be aware of the environment, at all times.

A house filled or surrounded with negative energy is one showing neglect. It is no different from the simple things of everyday life, like our wardrobe, which needs to be kept up to date so not to appear tired or neglected, and this care affects our inner and outer energy fields.

Good fun schway... says Grannie!

***

Supportive energy is achieved when there is a *clear space* in front of the building with a slow moving winding road (or sidewalk) nearby and not high-speed traffic.

Shapes: When a building's shape is not perfectly square or rectangle, consider landscaping this missing area with plants of bright monochromatic colors. *West* areas would be planted in white or pastel shades while empty *South* locations would be in red or pink tones. To complete, you can also identify the missing space with lights to square it up as part of the structure.

Renovation Change of energy can occur after renovating a building, when the overall shape has been altered from an addition. Noted changes could affect health (east sector) & relationships (southwest sector), especially if the new configuration becomes L-shaped creating a missing corner.

Metal wind chimes diminish ones financial source if located in the *southeast...* consider wood or black colored chimes.

Garage locations can be damaging to finances, especially if located in the Wealth area of the home (southeast). Make sure this area is in immaculate condition and always clean out unwanted items and garbage weekly.

Outside mailboxes are usually a 'metal' item. Enhance them with prosperity such as gold lettering to attract good fortune.

The occupants of *buildings that lack a strong foundation* could find themselves 'losing' money by not being totally grounded.

Garden areas: a birdbath invites the flow of positive energy if located in the North, East or Southeast sectors and increases prosperity.

Protective energy to a building can be achieved with 'plantings' around the back and sides providing a protective entrance.

Health: daily contact with nature cleanses the soul. Care for your garden. Walk barefoot in the grass.

Add healthy elements to the garden with herbs and food in the *east* sector.

The five *elements* (wood, earth, metal, water and fire) should be contained in the landscape design either with color or shapes. These balances produce harmony and enhance a sense of well-being for the occupants.

Earth elements: Place statues, rocks and stone items in the *southwest* and *northeast* sectors of the garden.

Harmonize the energy with *sound* in the garden; but beware that 'chimes' don't become annoying causing anxiety.

Water elements such as ponds, fountains and streams can destroy personal growth and achievements when situated in the south sector of the yard/garden. Keep them in the north.

Cleansing the garden creates room for abundance; remove weeds, twigs, branches and dead blossoms regularly so relationships in work and at home stay nourished and strong.

Increased opportunities come to a building with well-defined walkways, landings, steps, decks and patios, which are constructed from natural elements.

Yard Care has no room for broken pots, tools (Feng Shui identifies them as weapons) debris, dirty steps/patios, damaged furniture, chipped paint, cracked pavers and walkways, which all deplete the growth energy for a harmonized environment and abundance.

Rake leaves and keep eaves-troughs cleaned out so things run smoothly, to make room for new growth and new energy to correct or heal the environment.

***

Creative Space

Boys and their toys.
The North American west coast has had a strong passion for hot-roddin' since the 1950s. Collecting an old car was not only a means of transportation, but it was the dream of the Collector to find that *first* car he owned. There are the boys who own several and those who worship only one. Their passion is always the same.

A detailed eye doesn't miss a scratch, rim, tale-light, knob, or trunk handle let alone the uniqueness of how it 'sits'. These boys can discuss a particular item for an hour or a new component for an afternoon. Their positive energy is unbelievably high and in harmony as they are able to finish each other's sentences regarding an engine detail before it's spoken.

The boys gather regularly: Jim, Vern, Ken, Larry, Dan, Bob, Ron not mention Murray, Al, Gord, Jack, Don, Andy, John, Cam. There's a new roadster in town and everyone is interested. The comradeship is amazing.

The buildings where these vehicles are created, for the most part, are totally positive energy. A space filled with a guys heart and soul. The art, love and inspiration that go into these colourful, shiny treasures are from the heart. I have visited a few, not to mention many. The law of attraction lingers over the space as one tool is lost and another found only to be put away at the end of the day. Design details arise from moments of hesitation, allowing their intuition unlimited expression. Few of these hot rods are ever duplicated because of the owners focus to create yet another unique feature.

The millennium brought back the *Rat Rod roadster* from the 1950s to popularity as the real street rod encouraged a new wave of creativity. Another reason to have two hot rods in the garage!

These guys are known to take numerous road-trips, which also run in harmony. Never a moment goes by when one downfall or faulty part isn't attended to by the whole. Their trips are (almost) never made without mishaps, but a wonderful encounter or new friendships develop from the experience.

The mystical movement of energy is ever present whether in the working garage or on the road. It's a true art form on a large scale. The creative design of each individual hot rod is of a magnitude like no other.

From California to British Columbia, impressive vehicles display themselves at car shows as thousands of spectators view these amazing art-forms as they gracefully rumble into position. An overwhelming sense of harmony flows through the environment as children and grandparent's enjoy their craft, but never to touch, as the *boys* embark on spotting yet another new skill, art, detail, or inspiration.

One soon learns that you never visit the *boy's* humble abode while he is working. One inquisitive question could lead to a history of car stories. The walls are covered with years of momentums and dreams from when a teenager. And, the personality of a *car guy* is one thing when with the boys, and yet quite different when with others. It all has to do with the creative energy that flows between them, as they each caress their vehicle as if a woman, contemplating yet another dream.

Good fun schway... says Grannie!

***

(Three)
ENVIRONMENTAL ELEMENTS

Environmental energy
can be altered by temperature,
lighting, scent, color and shapes.

***

Form School teaches that houses built on hills, where the land slopes away, could be a draining factor on the occupants wealth (loss of needed positive energy).

Pa Kua: eight trigrams which form the basis of *I Ching* that make up the 64 hexagrams that surround the yin-yang round symbol.

Earth's energy field changes yearly.
You carry the earth's energy of your birth year with you all your life. 1948 was a Yang Earth energy year; 1960 was a Yang Metal-energy year; 1973 was a Yin Water-energy year; 1995 was a Yin Wood-energy year and 2007 was a Yin Fire-energy year, etc.

All birth years ending in an **even** number carry yang energy.
All birth years ending in an **odd** number carry yin energy.
Birth years ending in 0-1 carry metal-energy.
Birth years ending in 2-3 carry water-energy.
Birth years ending in 4-5 carry wood-energy.
Birth years ending in 6-7 carry fire-energy.
Birth years ending in 8-9 carry earth-energy.

***

Feng Shui is the use of Natural Products from earth's energy elements.

The Five Elements:

Water enhances Wood
Wood enhances Fire
Fire creates Earth
Earth produces Metal
Metal holds Water

***

Elements

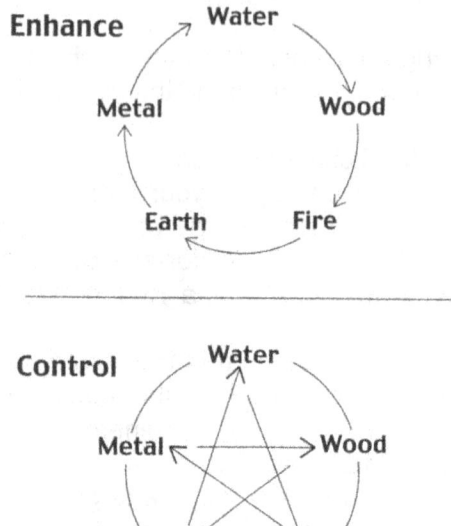

Each compass designation (Sector) carries the energy of an *Element*.

North - Water enhanced by (metal)
Northeast - Earth enhanced by (fire)
East - Wood enhanced by (Water)
Southeast - Wood enhanced by (Water)
South - Fire enhanced by (Wood)
Southwest - Earth enhanced by (Fire)
West - Metal enhanced by (Earth)
Northwest - Metal enhanced by (Earth)

***

Each compass designation (Sector) carries a *Life Aspiration* energy. A building has eight divides known as sectors.

North - Career Sector – the Journey
Northeast - Knowledge Sector
East - Health * Family Sector
Southeast - Wealth * Abundance Sector
South - Fame * Personal Recognition
Southwest - Relationships Sector
West - Creativity * Children Sector
Northwest - Travel * Friendships

***

Each compass designation (Sector) carries *Color* energy.

North - black - blue
Northeast - yellow - brown
East - teal to green
Southeast - greens
South - pink to red
Southwest - brown to yellow
West - grey, pastel to white
Northwest - pastel – grey

***

Each compass designation (Sector) carries *Shape* energy

North - irregular zig-zag shapes
Northeast – square - rectangle shape
East - vertical shape
Southeast - stripe - column shape
South - diamond - triangle shape
Southwest - rectangle - square
West - round-oval
Northwest - oval-round shapes

***

Each compass designation (Sector) carries energy of a *Number*. Lo Shun or magic square, as well as a color. This is the PaKua reading.

	SOUTH	
Wood **4** Green	Fire **9** Red	Earth **2** Yellow
Wood **3** Green	Earth **5** Yellow	Metal **7** White/Metallic
Earth **8** Yellow	Water **1** Black/Dark Blue	Metal **6** White/Metallic

North - one
Northeast - eight
East - three
Southeast - four
South - nine
Southwest - two
West - seven
Northwest - six
Centre - five

From the ancient *magic square,* all numbers placed on a 9 square grid total 15, vertically, horizontally and diagonally. South is located at the top centre square location.

***

Insight 'energy' found in Nature and the Environment through **color and numbers. (+** means positive; and **-** means negative attributes)

Black has + protection, birth and - sacrifice, secretiveness
Grey has + initiation and - imbalance
White has + purity, truth and - overextended, scattered

Violet has + alchemy, spirit and - obsession, misunderstood
Blue has + happiness, truth and - depression, loneliness
Brown has + new growth and - lack of discrimination
Green has +healing, abundance and - greed, miserly
Yellow has + inspiration and - over criticalness
Orange has + creativity, joy and - agitation, worry
Red has + sex, strength and - anger, impulse

Make note of any resemblance when you are surrounded or wearing these colors and your feelings.

***

Insight '*number* energy'
One has + beginnings and - arrogance
Two has + dreams, cooperation and - meddling
Three has + creativity, new birth and - gossip, moody
Four has + patience and - stubbornness
Five has + versatile, change and - overindulgent
Six has + family, home and - worrisome, jealous
Seven has + truth, wisdom and - critical, faithless
Eight has + power, money and - greedy, authoritarian
Nine has + understanding and - gullible, hypersensitive

***

People carry the **element-energy** of their birth year, all their life. Example traits for a male born in 1967.

yin fire-energy of the earth = environmental outer energy
wood   (the parent enhancement energy)
water (the grandparent control energy)
earth (the child, producing energy)
metal   (the weakening energy)

West person = best location is in a *west* building
Sheep = zodiac animal
Diamond, pointed items = *shape* energy
Reds = *color* energy
Number 6 *Pa Kua:* inner Intuitive natal energy (yang-west-metal-white)
Northwest = good *luck* location
Best directions to face = west, southwest, northeast, northwest

The above calculations say the man's outer-environmental, materialistic energy is *fire* and his inner spiritual energy is *metal*. According to the element flow chart, *fire* controls *metal*, thereby making it weaker. This person would tend to be stronger on his materialistic desires than using his intuition. To enhance his inner energy to amplify wisdom, he would need to add *earth* energy.

***

All of the (above) particulars are informative traits you incorporate into your life when there is a correction needed for harmony, balance and well-being. *Feng Shui, Lo Shun* and *I Ching* are about energy; a fact.

Could there be thousands of combinations from these calculations? (depending on each individual's birth date) Consider the 12 zodiac animals, five natural elements, yin or yang, male or female, twelve astrological signs, not to forget prosperous numbers, colors, best directions/locations etc. All this information lets you know what to incorporate into your life when you need a correction for harmony, revitalization, etc.

These signs have all been calculated from your birth date.

***

Fire elements would be items of a pyramid, diamond, triangle shape; flame patterns; candles; lights; skylites; fireplaces; barbques; colors of red, pink, terra cotta, burgundy. Bright lights on dimmer switches keep the energy controlled, especially in entrances, dining area, study areas and dark hallways for safety and clarity.

Earth elements
would include pottery, ceramic, china, crystal, granite, marble, slate, stone, brick, gemstones, garden art; mountain landscapes, shapes of items square or rectangle and colors of yellows, brown, beige.

Water elements
would be irregular shapes; colors that are deep dark, black and items such as shells, fish, water, ocean landscapes and fountains.

Metal elements
would be shapes that are oval or round; colors of pastels, gray and white; and items of silver, gold, iron, copper, brass, metallic.

Wood elements
can be positive energy in the southeast Wealth sector when using stripe wall coverings, green or teal colored paints, fabrics or natural wood furnishings are Wood elements.

***

Every *person*, based on their personal *(Pa Kua)* Energy charts calculated from their birth year, is either a *West* or *East* Person. These calculations also indicate a person's four most prosperous *locations* to be situated in when working, eating, and sleeping, etc.

Keeping the Balance: the Feng Shui concept of collaborating the occupant's energy charts with their buildings energy charts as every *building* carries the energy of the *direction in which the front door faces.*

Every building is either an *East* or a *West* building depending on the location where it '*sits*'.

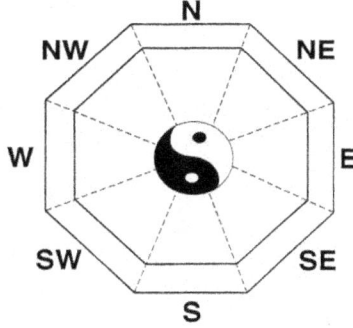

Natural elements carry the most positive flow of energy; very prosperous and healthy to the environment. Wood or tile floors are superior to synthetics, laminates, vinyls, carpeting etc. that carry excessive volatile chemicals and off-gas.

Wood elements would be items vertical in shape; (stripes) green, aqua, teal in color; botanical items, rattan, hemp, cotton, floral fabrics; plants; organic items; furniture; natural fiber carpets; art items; drapery panels.

Energy *change* is accomplished through color, shapes or an element item (fire=lamp) which can actually introduce significant changes.

In Feng Shui concepts, a list of seven *aspects* recommended for every room. They include: life – light – stillness – sound – movement – color – meandering path = harmony

Remedies for the balance of energy in a room.
    life = plant.
    sound = music or clock.
    stillness = statue or vase.
    color = art or wallpaper.
    movement = patterned fabric, drapery.
    light = lamps, windows.
    meandering energy paths = (no straight lines).

Elements:
Limestone is an excellent source of 'earth' energy when placed in <u>west</u> entries/rooms.

China or pottery placed near a <u>water</u> element (artwork or fountain) in the 'north' sector can bring about mishaps & problems within the career.

***

**Enhancement and Control
Element Remedies.**

A very confusing part of the Feng Shui exercise is the *Energy Charts*. Each person in a family has their own specific energy information, and this information is carried with you *all the years of your life*. If you are an *East* person, with prosperous locations of south, east, north and southeast, and you spend over half million dollars or more on a property, it would be wise to see that its energy is compatible to yours. Everyone has at one time or another, found certain places '*not to their liking*'. Your inner sense, gut feeling or intuition tells you, and you want to leave before taking a complete look at the premise. This 'knowing' is a reaction or warning against *negative energy* that you are feeling.

There are times when you feel uncomfortable around certain people, and don't want to be working with them, even though you have not really met them or worked with them before. Your energies are not blending, so to speak.

The mystical movement of energy works with you, if you are focused, or aware of its warnings. Even if a house is carrying *East* energy and you are a *West* person, there are always corrections that can be applied through the realignment of natural elements to enhance the prosperity of the building to suit you. This balancing of Yin and Yang principals puts the environment in harmony. You may have visited a location and had a good feeling about it. Perhaps it wasn't your taste in decoration, but it just '*felt*' good. Some restaurants can give you that same feeling.

Exercise.
One of the best ways to find out if you are living in your best energy field, is to analyze, in detail, the room where *you* spend the most time.

To do this, you need a compass to find out its location within the building. If you are an *East* person, and the room is located in the northwest, you would probably be best *sitting* or *working* in the north or south sectors, which are good energy spots for you. You may want to *face* east or southeast when working, or watching TV. Moving yourself into new positions when things are out of sorts will change the energy flow (of the room) around you. Always change the energy when things aren't going your way. Drive to work a different route. Sleep on the opposite side of the bed. Sit in another chair. Enter the building from another entrance than the usual one.

Carry your birth year element-energy with you, perhaps on a key chain for good fortune. If you are a Yin Wood, perhaps a piece of wood with a whale (fish) on it as water enhances wood; if you carry the energy of Yang Metal, perhaps a round metal shape with a gemstone in it, etc.

Some people, places, rooms, buildings feel comfortable when you are in and around them because you found your positive energy field that is compatible to your 'birth year' energy that you carry with you all your life. You know if it is good or bad for you from your intuition and the way you perform. *'Attention* to *detail'* is recommended to keep yourself healthy, creatively inspired and in good relationships. Be aware of others who feed-off or take your energy, leaving you tired and lethargic. Stay away from this negative energy.

Good fun schway... says Grannie!

***

Locations: Beware of the element 'wood', which controls/damages 'earth' (which is representative of 'relationships') in the southwest. Relocate any greenery items located in this area of a room so not to dominate and weaken the positive energy.

Electronics are 'metal' items and weaken one's health when placed in the east, which is the 'wood' element location. Consider a new location for these items and strengthen the family/health area with a water element or the color 'black'.

'White' is the energy-color for the element 'metal' and should be limited in the east area of the room/building so it isn't a weakening factor to the 'health' of the occupants.

'Water' elements are best located in the north representing the Career aspiration for abundance and achievements.

Personal recognition – south sector, should be free of any black objects near lamps or windows so not to weaken one's goals.

Too much dark Yin colors such as black, brown, navy can create a 'depressed' state, psychologically and need to be balanced with 'yang' light colors for a state of harmony.

Color: Balance is accomplished when using both warm and cool colors in the same palate.

***

Fun with Travel – Student Moves

There are numerous ways to have fun schway in everyday life. It wasn't that long ago that Kim, a close friend of my daughters, was interested in traveling, but she always had some kind of mishaps.

She had traveled to England and worked briefly as a Nanny, but had to return due to illness. Another trip took her to Spain, and no sooner did she arrive then she returned to the west coast. It didn't seem to matter where she travelled, something always came up to ruin her trip or experience. We chatted about it on numerous occasions and I suggested we should try something to attract some good fortune.

Kim was living in a small apartment where she studied, lived and slept all in one room, more or less. It was a tight place, to say the least.

Together, we spent some time preparing her Energy charts, based on her birth year. They indicated that she carried the energy of Yang Metal, and she was an East person. I did a compass reading on her apartment, finding it a West house (so to speak). We needed to apply a few corrections.

With an enlightened attitude, Kim restructured her tiny space. It was in need of a clean out, as everything needed reorganizing. Several books and school papers from years past had to be stored elsewhere. The old material wasn't required for her current semester and had to go. She was also applying to different Universities anticipating a possible move, which was giving her more reason to clear out her things. The tiny closet would provide more space and every inch counted. Change the energy and change your life!

With little income, other than her 20 hours a week working at the Gap, Kim put together some unique shelving units that covered a whole wall and painted them the same color as the wall, a soft olive green. Her daybed also needed to blend into the color of the walls, so to fade away and create a space visually looking larger. The throw-cover she found matched perfectly. This helped reduce the size of the bed by camouflaging it into the background, making the room feel more spacious.

Numerous large wicker baskets were stacked for needed storage. A small drop-leaf table was painted white, along with the 2 stools. We added white toss pillows for the daybed. Lots of organization. Nothing went on the walls except a very large bulletin board (corkboard) for all her scattered paper-clutter that she would now control. Kim needed the *head* of her daybed to face one of her 4 best directions for sleeping, and being an East person, the room only allowed for one spot that was free of doors or windows. We placed it so her head would face North. She felt comfortable with that.

We discussed her next step. Out came the compass, and the notepaper. She felt the energy within the room change, becoming more Zen.

The aspiration 'Travel' is located in the northwest sector (compass). Kim wanted extra money for her trip, so she needed to enhance the 'Wealth' sector, which is the southeast section of the room.

The small space needed to be as empty as we could possibly make it because she needed the incoming energy to be attracted to these particular sectors for enhancement.

After plotting her room onto a plan, which we identified by compass directions, we learned that the entry door to her place was in the Travel sector. The northwest sector carries the energy of metal. This would be a difficult area to enhance. We decided to search for a collage of photos and frame them in chrome, artistically, which would identify her travel. Photos of airplanes, travel location, good weather, etc were all gathered and applied onto a white (metal color) board and framed.

The only place we could place this was on the wall behind the entry door. Beneath the collection of pictures, I placed her empty suitcase (which happened to be grey, which is a metal color) with her affirmation statement written out and placed inside. She identified in detail her desired trip.

After that, we located the Wealth sector of the room where she had placed the long shelf unit. This had been organized with baskets, books, CD's, photos etc. By leaving a clear section open for a grouping of plants, she added several violets (which were affordable.) The Wealth sector carries the energy of wood, so plants would enhance the area. I wanted her to place a *toonie* ($2.00 coin) into one of the plants... the idea was to encourage growth when she wrapped it in red silk. She located a small crystal vase and filled it with distilled water. Kim had received it as a gift and set it in between the plants to enforce their growth as water feeds wood energy.

Everything appeared and felt better in her space and she felt happier studying and living there.

Several weeks passed before I received a call from Kim. She was struggling with her exams, work and relationships. This was due to the shift in energy. We met for coffee the following week. By this time, she appeared in good spirits as the energy calmed.

The new ever-changing energy that came into her life was big, she explained. When it settled, the exams had gone well and she received a small raise from her work. She didn't say anything about the relationship, so I thought better not to mention it. Kim was in good spirits now. She was accepted at a University in Quebec and was preparing for a new venture to Montreal.

Just days before she was to fly east, Kim received an unexpected call from friends who wanted her to travel south to the Cayman Islands with them. No expenses. It wasn't her dream trip to the Canary Islands, but it ended up being better than she could have ever dreamed.

Kim graduated McGill University, went on to get a Masters in Women Studies, and then was accepted for her PHD study at University of Toronto at only 24 years old.

Today, she still loves to travel, keeping her *toonie* in her violets in the southeast sector of her room.

Good fun schway... says Grannie!

***

Color: Blues should be limited in boardrooms and bedrooms because it is a 'water' representation and can have a draining effect on the space. Blue can be combined with 'earth' colors yellow/beige to 'control' its *moving* effects. (Earth dams water).

Shapes: Square or rectangle shapes are prosperous when located in the northeast or southwest (earth representations) when selecting door, windows, tables, planters, patios, mirrors, art, carpets etc.

Oval or round shapes are prosperous when located in the west area of a room when used as tables, mirrors, art, rugs, planters, plates, or in fabric prints.

Shift in energy: Consider round mirrors in the west; and square mirrors in the southwest; vertical mirrors in the east.

Not coping well with life's changes can be from too much black (water element) as one seeks the dark; winter. Add touches of red (fire) or white(metal) to the space or your wardrobe where the dark dominates.

Fear is cleansed with metal/water (black/white) corrections. Areas of bladder, kidney, ears, bones, head, hair.

Anger is cleansed (wood/water) greens/blues. Areas of nails, eyes, liver, gallbladder corrections.

Joy is done with fire/wood (red/greens). Areas of heart, intestines corrections.

Negative 'bad luck' energies happen when items of fire or earth elements are in the north sector.

Negative 'bad luck' energies happen when items of water or metal elements are in the south sector.

Negative 'bad luck' energies happen when items of fire and wood elements are in the west sector

Negative 'bad luck' energies happen when items of earth or metal elements are in the east sector.

(Four)
AWARENESS

Multi-tasking is the ability to fill up time
and space so that **you** don't.
Time becomes rigid in routine.
Be conscious of all things you do.

***

An East building is considered to SIT (location) in *East* energy in the east, southeast, north, and south sectors. This means the front entry door faces the direction of north, south, west or northwest as the *location* is found on the opposite side of the (compass) facing direction. The most prosperous East building is when the facing direction of the entry is either north or south (when looking out from the inside) because this is the 'only' direction and location combination that carry east-energy for both facing and sitting.

A West building is considered to SIT (location) in *West* energy in the west, southwest, northwest and northeast sectors. This means the front entry door faces the opposite direction towards southeast, southwest, east or northeast. The most prosperous West building has the facing direction of the entry towards southwest or northeast when looking out from the inside because this is the 'only' direction and location combination that carry west-energy for both facing and sitting.

Fun Schway Interiors appearance have hidden agendas... dust mirrors and clean windows, and all glass surfaces 'regularly' to keep away all impurities.

Interior life-elements; greenery should be cared-for by removing dead leaves & blossoms; such as to remove old baggage that drags us down,

Walk your premises regularly, and take note of any damage, wear, required repairs or touch-ups. As soon as identified, immediately attend to the damages to prevent illness from entering.

Corners should *not* be left empty as the energy becomes trapped and stagnant. This can cause forgetfulness for the occupants. Place a loved item or greenery in this area.

Hallways are a concern.
Reduce fast flowing energy within long corridors/hallways with the placement of plants, furniture, moldings, sconces, art or other items to maintain balance within the building.

Interior observation: Make note that *negative* rooms are wet rooms; i.e. bathrooms, kitchens, and laundry (storage) rooms.

Holding onto the Past: Remove all unwanted presents/gifts & hand-me-downs that are not completely loved, no matter where they came from. They hold energy that vibrates and takes up space, where it is better to have nothing, leaving room for 'special' items.

Overhead awareness for restrictions such as hanging objects that can gather dust, restrict energy flow and encourage stagnation, not to mention ... forgetfulness.

Neglect: Don't neglect any room in the building. All spaces must be nurtured, as avoiding cold, junk and neglected areas will only reduce productivity and progress.

Cleansing: Remove negative energies from a room after an argument, unwanted guests, sickness, quarrels, romantic breakup by lighting a candle, playing favorite music and doing a thorough cleanse of the space.

Interior Entry is the location where the building 'inhales' the energy at its front door; therefore, this area needs cleansing and enhancement with a flowing, flowering plant or floral bouquet for beauty. This location should never face trash, polluted waters, or anything damaged or broken.

The entry is a place of 'welcoming' and should be free from clutter so the positive energy can circulate freely. Place something *special* in this space.

Entry doors are *not* to face onto a staircase especially if the stairs are split (level) going both up and down, which is the worst configuration creating some complications for all those living in the building. This is an area where you hang wind chimes between the doorway and the stairs.

Foyers should *never* have a mirror (reflective surface) *'opposite'* the entry door as it deflects the incoming positive energy back out, which can add 'difficulties' to the buildings prosperity.

Entries should be free from obstruction especially behind the entry door so not to bring hardships into the 'welcoming' area of the building.

Foyers need movement to encourage the energy and this is a very good location for wall coverings that has movement in its pattern. The same idea works well for carpeting or rugs.

Interior entry area should be free from bathrooms, which can 'flush' the incoming positive energy down the drain.

The entry location should be free of windows located opposite the entry door to the building, as the energy will flow in and out of the building quickly leaving the building without any prosperity.

***

Improvement in Health

One extremely hot summer's day in August comes to mind when discussing health issues. A client of mine in the decorating industry operated a family owned business. Roy Kuziw was a very active individual with a great personality. I couldn't believe my ears when I visited his shop to find out from staff, that he was no longer coming in due to poor health. In fact, it was a lot worse than poor health.

I soon learned that he not only had cancer, open-heart surgery and several angina attacks, but also had experienced TIAs numerous times. I contacted his daughter who was a client, made inquiries, and then said I would like to speak to him as soon as he was able.

His situation remained on my mind during the following weeks. I needed to place an order with them, so again I visited the shop. His wife Dorothy was working that particular Tuesday. We had a brief chat about my order for custom hardware. When she inquired about upcoming Feng Shui seminars, I said I would email her some information, and then proceeded to make inquiries about Roy. We decided to meet for lunch the following week.

It was early September when we met at the Selkirk restaurant on the waterfront. We ordered beverages and took some time before looking at the menu for lunch. I asked about any mishaps over the past year.

Roy explained to me in detail the complications he experienced. It was just mind boggling to hear it all, and to see how his health had deteriorated. I suggested that we look at their home together to see if there were any corrections that could be made for a quicker recovery. They were ready to try any solution, so we made plans to meet the next day. I hadn't realized that their accommodations were above their workshop; a renovation they did 18 months beforehand.

I arrived early afternoon and we did a quick walk-thru the apartment. I learned that he had started to fail shortly after the renovations were completed. Before they had moved onto the premise, they both were reasonably well. I applied the compass to the entry, learning that the unit was considered a *'West'* House because the entry door faced northeast, therefore the house 'sat' in a westerly location, being southwest.

According to the Energy charts of Roy, he was an *East* person. Not a great beginning! We walked to the bedroom location where we could apply some realignment to encourage a healthier space for Roy.

The most important issue in a *health* correction is to allow as much positive energy as possible to reach the occupants sleeping in the room. In this particular case, the bedroom location was in the northeast sector, (not great for Roy). Negative energy was apparent all through the room. The head of the bed was on the west wall, (his Total Loss sector, known as 'chueh ming' location). The bed was covered with a decorative canopy, which had to be removed to open up the space allowing more healing energy to reach him. Nothing over your head is essential.

There were numerous knickknacks along a ledge behind the bed, which needed clearing off, as less is best for healing energy. The artwork located on the wall behind the headboard had to be removed so not to interfere with the flow of positive energy.

There were two corner-walls (sharp edges) protruding directly at him when in bed – a noted poison arrow. Over-decorated windows with drapery, blinds and valances needed scaling down to allow more Fire-energy into the room from the windows.

A twelve-foot wall of sliding mirror doors (which is a real no-no in the bedroom) had to be attended to. They represent Water-energy (reflective surface) and too much movement, constantly activating the energy when it needs to be meandering and remain calm. This is not a healing element. I didn't get to see much of the rest of their home, but by the look on his face, he appeared delighted and encouraged..

We immediately began to clear out the room of excess furnishings and items that could go elsewhere or be removed completely. We relocated the bed so he no longer faced the bathroom door. He was now in his *'best location'* (according to his Energy chart) and had a commanding view of the entry door to the bedroom.

Both Dorothy and Roy agreed to apply wall coverings onto the sliding mirrored doors. A new paint color was selected in a 'suede finish' for less shine and drama, in a more neutral healing shade. The flowered bedding cover (wood-energy) would be replaced with a 'less patterned' fabric in a tone that blended into the wall color so not to add any busyness to the room and the bed (coloring) would fade away into the wall color to keep the space as calm as possible. The bathroom door needed to stay closed at all times; all drains plugged and the toilet seat kept down. Bathrooms are negative spaces with soil, dirty water, etc and must be closed off from the occupants for protection.

Several hours later, we finished with some recommendations for the rest of their unit. I explained it was not great energy for the bedroom to be located over the garage. Something to remember. I also suggested he change the position of his seating at the dining table, so he would sit in one of his more prosperous locations. It was a long, tiring day, but I knew the shift in energy flow would help him.

By early December, I received a message to pick up some products I had ordered at Roy's shop. I ventured over to find him back at work and looking much better. He couldn't believe how energetic he felt, explaining that all the medications he had been on finally felt like they were working. This was good news to hear, that by removing the negative energy from his environment, he began to heal and receive a more positive flow. Now, I told him... *clean up your desk!* He laughed, but he did do this because he knew that when the outward environmental energy was changed, then his inward healing could begin. A good sign was he enlisted into Yoga breathing exercises, reducing a stressful lifestyle.

Time and time again, we gather 'things' that carry energy that are not compatible to ours, and over the years they become negative and dominate our wellness, and we begin to lose harmony. Always get rid of *too much* within your environment. Routine is not good and change will always revitalize the soul.

Good fun schway... says Grannie!

***

An *East* person needs to heal in an east room when sick, just as a *West* person needs to recover in a west room for successful cures.

Harmful plants are those with spiky leaves or prickly plant (cactus- keep these out of the dining area.)

Relationships: Two natural crystals located side by side add to the 'love luck' in the southwest sector.

Lack of Inspiration: Fireplaces are a 'fire' element and so is the color red, candle groupings; large windows – when located on a *west wall* as they can decrease/stagnate the aspiration 'Creativity – Children'.

Correction to staircases: if located facing the entry door, the strong downward flowing energy needs to slowdown and this is accomplished by placing a small mirror at the bottom of the stairs to reflect it.

Yin & Yang balance:
Hard & soft flooring; warm & cool colors; high & low ceilings; dark & light furniture are the yin/yang of the interior and therefore must harmonize.

Protective energy is achieved by camouflaging a poor (window) view with a beautiful covering, which still provides the needed light.

Safety: Lower your stress level. Make note of any loose, sliding carpets causing dangerous space when sloppy.

Caution of overhead fans.
Make them disappear into the color of the ceiling and go unseen and blend out-of-sight so they don't drain the positive, prosperous energy.

Wall groupings can have too many items, which depicts confusion and signals imbalance of energy affecting friendships and relationships. Your thoughts and focus can become weaker, like obstacles getting into the way.

Good communication and space planning allows for 8'0" maximum space between cross seating-distance for a balanced flow that is harmonized. (Knee to knee when sitting comfortably.)

Tiredness, laziness can be a sign of stagnant energy. Clear off the windowsills; remove blockage that hinders light coming into the space, and then open the window.

Interior Lighting must be in good working order at all times, making sure no burnt out bulbs, broken switches, cracks or damages are repaired as 'lights' are a 'fire' element and need power to boost the energy forward.

Colorful bowls of fruit situated on tables are an excellent 'life' element expressing abundant energy, only to attract more.

Electronic devices such as TV, computers and stereos represent the element 'metal' and therefore should not be placed in the east area of a room (wood) because *metal cuts wood* (controls it) so that the room would resonate with negative energy and a depletion of finances could develop.

***

Universal Flow & Electromagnetic Fields

Multi-tasking was the 'jargon' beginning back in the 1980s for Super-Moms and stay-at-home Dads in the 1990s. But, I had a few clients that could not cope with it all.

When it came time to visit their home, it was like a last cry for help. It was plain to see that the last twenty years of a high-pace lifestyle in the Western world had produced a hectic home life for many families. The pace has not slowed at all.

Houses and offices were jammed packed with everyday '*stuff*' that never found a home-for-itself. Everyone *appeared* to be taken care of... the meals wee made, the kids got to their sport events, school, piano lessons, or whatever else they were involved with, but the stress level of multi-tasking appeared quite high. Things never got put away. Laundry was another story.

Today is no different. No one seems to have time for a leisurely lunch or dinner, let alone breakfast. The organic foods, counting-carbs and cholesterol-free items just don't matter for many families. Fast food meals are what fit into the time slot between schedules. There is no time. The house actually feels stressed-out everywhere I look. However, there's usually one room kept orderly where nobody goes into much, just in case someone visits.

It feels as if everyone in the family is talking at once, and no one is actually listening. Pets, phones and visitors are coming and going all at once. Do you know any family like this?

I remember in Europe how everyone seemed to have two-hour lunches, and shops closed so that all experienced conversation, good food and relaxation. They had a balance of leisure time. However, when 'our society takes a breather', our minds are still racing with thoughts of so many 'things' that need doing, or stuff not to forget, that even our quiet times become stressful.

Our environment (outward) reacts similar to our thoughts (inward). Laws of attraction, *like attracts like* are the same for our personal space as it is for our inner thoughts.

If our surroundings are busy with lots of *stuff*, then it attracts a busy, cluttered mind. A Zen, calm space attracts a clear, productive mind. We are what we see.

The energy that surrounds us, is a reflection of what's inside of us. Negative, sloppy, messiness attracts more complications into our life. Therefore, if any items are broken, then mishaps happen (*like attracts like*). Less is best and this is one of the reasons why some people seem to be over-active and continually multi-tasking. Check and see if your environment is full of '*stuff*', especially in cupboards, garage, basements, attics, etc.

I have worked with clients and seen several boxes in their garage or basement that they tell me have never been opened, but keep moving them from house to house. If they are never opened or used every few months, get rid of the old baggage, and feel less burdened. The boxes are most likely full of '*stuff*' that isn't even wanted, let alone needed.

Our *negative* thoughts attract 'more' wrong, unhappiness because the flow of (*positive*) energy doesn't recognize any *negative words*. If you say... I **don't** want to live like this anymore... you will have a difficult time changing, because '*negative* thoughts and words' do *not* register within the *positive* energy field; therefore, *energy* reads it as... *I* **want** to live like this... so many of our wishes never come to pass. Everything you think or say that has negative words in it, will be interpreted *without* those words because the Positive energy wants to reach you, and therefore will not compute them. *Like attracts like* and your inner positive energy wants to attract the same.

Warning. Be careful *not* to agree with others when they speak negative. People can take your energy and you will feel drained.

You cannot *see* electricity, or the wind, or music, but you understand its benefits and feel it, knowing it is there. Quantum Physics notes that everything is vibrating and has motion. There are sounds that our pets hear, but we don't hear. It is the mystical movement of energy that we don't see, but know that it is there.

Whenever 'wrong' comes into your life, rethink the actual words you said or thought, and then look around your environment. It is all interconnected. If the environment is out of harmony, likely so is your busy mind, which can deprive you of needed sleep.

Where do we begin... is the comment from many families. Before healing, calm your insides. You will feel a whole lot better when you start with your environment first. If you see and feel harmony, make better decisions, and then you will be calmer and so will everyone else within the space.

Begin at the beginning. Be and stay organized. Set schedules for everyone and everything. For positive movement of energy, there has to be space for its movement. Nothing can be in the way, on the floor, on tables, dressers, behind entry doors. Think clearly, create clarity. Focus on meditation to stop the chattering mind or it will dominate your decisions.

Be healthier by being outdoors more. Enjoy nature and let it nurture your soul. Find your own quiet space for half-hour every single day and breathe deeply three times beforehand when feeling stressed or just go for a walk. This time and space alone will refresh you so decisions will be easier and you will find everything less stressful. You will soon find the need *not* to multi-task. Once the positive energy reaches you, a sense of well-being and calm enters your life. Even a soft color scheme can affect your environment.

We all collect 'away too much stuff" which somehow reflects back on us with 'away too much thinking' (busy mind) and we need to reduce as well as relax. A need for clarity is a need to live a more Zen life. It is much healthier.

Take two-hour lunches without guilt; enjoy good healthy food, conversation, family and friends. Forget the TV, video game, radio, computer, etc. That's what positive energy flow is all about. Feel it!

Good fun schway... says Grannie!

***

By making more empty space, this will present opportunities. Remove 'throws, pillows and stuff from table tops, excess art and accessories', always leaving at least 50% of all surfaces empty... so there is ample room for the energy of new opportunities and happiness to enter.

Enhancing the Sector:
From the ancient Vedic science of India, *Spiritual knowledge* is your inner intuition and this sector is found in the northeast area. VAASTA says 'never stay in this sector more than a few hours' so its energy is always free from obstruction.

Careers can be 'kick-started' when taking the element of the sector (water) and combining it with its enhancing element (metal) sid-by-side. Water elements (fountains, water art, shells, black/navy colors) combined with anything (white/gray colors or round shapes) metal objects are placed together in a clear area in the north sector for Career enhancements. Kick it up a notch!

Financial distress can begin to turn around when the wood elements (plants, but not overgrown) are situated in the southeast area next to a water element (fountain), in a 'clear corner' so the incoming energy can enhance its vibrations. Place $$ under the pot wrapped in red silk. Good fun schway.

Living/Family rooms & reception areas require all five natural elements because of the variety of people who enter, to keep the energy in balance and accommodating for everyone. These elements must be placed in their specified areas... such as wood elements in the east; water elements in the north; fire elements in the south, etc.

Dining areas or eating spaces should be separate from the working kitchen as kitchens negative energy can affect the occupant's digestion.

Interior dining or eating spaces can be damaging to health when located beneath a bathroom (on the floor above) as family nourishment becomes *pressed down* by negative energy. Put an up-lite fixture on the ceiling to control this energy.

Enhance the dining sector by placing a mirror opposite the dining table, which is a symbol of doubling abundance for the occupants. Restaurants that use them tend to be prosperous.

Dining area artwork should be an expression of abundance, lushness, symbolizing wealth, longevity & good fortune.

Each person sitting at a dining table should face one of his or her four best directions when eating to enhance good health.

The centre of the dining table is an earth representation and can be enhanced with... crystal, ceramic, pottery or glass, next to candles.

Never eat food from any off-gassing surface such as plastic, Teflon or chemically treated surfaces. Discard all plastic, styrofoam containers that cause disease and poor health as these harmful chemicals are showing up in DNA.

A dining table: enhanced with high back chairs are supportive while low back seating leaves the occupant unsupported & vulnerable, especially when their back is to an open doorway.

Tables that are round or oval are conducive to positive energy and friendly flowing energy for discussions when used regularly.

A rooms lighting usually suggests the triangle of three lamps for adequate 'fire' element situated near corners of the room.

Lighting (fire element) is recommended in Tri-lite products for well lit spaces offering three stages of brightness, so as the occupant is in control of this powerful element.

Furnishings: Round or demilune windows and tables are prosperous on the west, north and northwest walls of a building to add creative energies to the room as well as enhancing friendships and travel.

Color enhancements need balance. Don't be 'bottom heavy' in texture and color, such as dark furniture without balancing the 'top' of the space for a sense of harmony with drapery rods or decorative moldings.

***

(Five)
RELATIONSHIPS

What you see in others is your own reflection.
Contemplate what their actions mean to you,
and what they are trying to tell you.

***

Location of your private rooms should be located the furthest distance from the front entry.

Avoid inappropriate relationships -
that sadden and drain your energy, which resonates in the space around you, wherever you go, attracting mishaps and negative energy.

Feng Shui recommends removing electronic items and toys from bedrooms... interferes with the earth's electromagnetic field, especially when sleeping.

Best Directions: sleep with the headboard of the bed facing your most prosperous direction (one of the four) remembering that everyone wakes up refreshed when they are situated in their best location – sheng ch'i.

Sleep: a good strong headboard provides maximum support, clarity of mind and a sound sleep.

Warning: don't place any items on the wall above the head of the bed, as the body needs all the positive energy it can get while sleeping.

Energy flow in the bedroom is enhanced when reflective surfaces are removed from the room, especially glass framed art and mirrors, as they activate the energy and the bedroom needs to remain calm.

Don't sit, eat, or sleep under an overhead light fixture (fire element)... subconsciously poses a threat with headaches, migraines, loss of focus, loss of vision, etc.

Don't sit, eat, work or sleep under overhead beams for any length of time. This is known to cause unwanted headaches, lack of creative thought, tiredness, anxiety and moodiness,

Masters recommend working, relaxing or sleeping is always healthier when facing your most prosperous direction known as 'sheng ch'i'.

Caution: reduce the number of living plants in the bedroom so not to use up oxygen; but they do assist in absorbing the off-gassing from carpets and other volatile materials and objects.

It is *not* recommended to sleep beneath a window (fire element) which can reduce 'support' and makes for a poor night sleep unless fully covered.

It is wise to have a clear view of the bedroom door from the bed, for you to remain in control.

Water elements are considered negative in the bedroom; therefore, en suite bathrooms should always have the door closed.

Bedroom doors should *not* line up or face another door across the corridor... conflicting energy patterns. This correction transpires with a strong 'up light' on the ceiling.

***

Communication

There is a magnetism created between two people when they are in balance. It is joyful, fun and good times. The principal of attraction when creating harmony happens when emotions and feelings are aroused both mentally or physically.

I carry with me a silver letter **M**, or is it **W**? It all depends on how you look at it. In ancient times, the creation of obelisks, pyramids and decorative wall art with triangles were plentiful. The upward point designated the *male, positive and 'giving'* energy, while the inverted triangle was the *female, negative and 'receiving' energy*. For me the letter **W** (with its centre point) represents the '*giving it*' but then another would look at this letter to represent the female with its two valleys, the double 'receiving it'. However, the **M** for me (with its centre valley) is the '*receiving it*' for the feminine energy. It's my yin/yang reminder for controlling my emotional energy.

When a discussion is taking place, there can be many pyramids, lots of '*giving it*' going on, and not a lot of valleys, '*receiving it*' energy and therefore we have arguments. There is no balance, therefore no resolution. We need more listeners. It's all about keeping the balance.

There must always be a balance of both energies for the perfect relationship. Great souls know intuitively when to exercise these energies as the 'pyramid' *male energy* is considered a temporary submission and distinctively more intellectual, while the 'valley' *female energy* that 'receives it' is non resistant with a sense of freedom and essentially spiritual, which acknowledges the impelling power while creating harmony through its wisdom. This combination is the human magnet.

The ancient sage was a person of wisdom who was the '*choiceless watcher*' who exercised knowingly, according to the requirements of the situation. We need to observe before we react. Compromise by paying attention to your own magnetic field of emotional energy.

You are able to control your conditions as you come to sense the purpose of what you attract by your vibrating emotions working positively or negatively around you. There is a time and place for positive (*giving it*) energy and a time for the negative (*receiving it*) energy that works to your advantage. When you are *giving* instructions, you are in the positive, and when *receiving* the instructions, you are in the negative. There are times when we need to be the *'choiceless watcher*, and just listen.

Realigning the romance area of the home is in the southwest sector of the bedroom and depending on the occupant's Energy charts there are good and bad locations for the bed. It is usually said that the person 'paying' for the household has the bed facing their best direction, and then the other person gets to pick which side of the bed is best for them. Compromise creates harmony.

When a breakup or separation has occurred, the first thing is to get rid of past energies. That means remove the personal items from bedding to gifts from the room, and then re energize it with new paint and realign the furnishings, if possible. A good cleansing of the space can enhance one's magnetic energy field.

Enhance new relationships with candles (two), artwork (two) and keep the number of pillows to a minimum on the bed in twos or you may be inviting unwanted people or incidents into your relationship. A single pillow may indicate you are satisfied being on your own.

Dan and Lorraine Knox who live in Riverside, California have two children. Lots of ups and downs raising children. Keeping things harmonious around the home does have its problems. The balance of positive (*male - giving it*) energy and negative (*female - receiving it*) energy is difficult in the best of times. It is only 'after' a situation happens that they can stand back and analyze who was in what energy field. Clearing the air is like clearing the room. When they get rid of the papers, toys, dishes, clothes, etc, they can actually feel the harmony of the environment, which resonates with their inner energy, and with their kids as well. The '*giver*' and '*receiver*' must listen, then, there is harmony. When there is harmony, there is love, laughter and kindness. Your environment is a reflection of your inner self.

A good exercise is to actually look back at your day and make note of how many times, in situations at work, home etc that you were carrying Yang (masculine) or Yin (feminine) energy in the relationships encountered. Were you 'giving it' or 'receiving it'. Maybe, it is time for you to carry the letter **M** on your key chain, or is it **W**?

Good fun schway... says Grannie!

***

NOTES:

Negative energy within the bedroom can have serious 'ill' effects. Be aware.

Feng Shui warns staircases should not line up with a bedroom door causing fast flowing energy to enter the room. This space is one that needs to be tranquil and calm, holding the positive energy in place.

Negative energy directed toward the bed would incorporate any clutter, poison arrows, and sharp corners, any damaged, broken or cracked items, especially in an L-shaped room.

Negative energy can come from open shelves (which should be covered just like mirrors at bedtime) as they cause damage, headaches & mishaps when aimed at the bed, not to mention a poor night's sleep.

Bad Luck: clutter in the bedroom can provoke bad luck and missed fortunes.

Feng Shui recommends that the bed should be clear from obstacles tucked beneath it that encourage aches, pains and difficult times.

For best results, do not have the bedroom entry door opposite or across from a window, otherwise the entering energy will flow directly out the window causing a loss of energy to the occupants' room, which can weaken ones creative intuition and relationships.

Wisdom: remember that the southwest section of the bedroom is the 'Relationship' area of the room and should be enhanced with 2 crystals; 2 red candles or 2 'loved' photos to strengthen its energy. Never have this space cluttered.

Loss: be aware of open fireplaces in the bedroom which can drain (or burn) much of the romance out of the relationship.

Weakening of a relationship comes from numerous pillows on the bed that could encourage others into the relationship. Consider sets of 'two' for a healthy relationship.

Good support: make sure a wall is behind the head of the bed. It is not a good idea to place the bed across a corner... lack of support, and situations can become weakened, allowing unexpected events to happen without any notice.

'Calming colors' won't accelerate energy flow into the space - recommended for extrovert children

Pick up *before* bedtime, as any 'clutter' adds to a disrupted sleep as does anything left on the floor. This negative energy can encourage nightmares.

The bedroom is for only sleeping, but if a study area is required, it is best situated in the northeast (knowledge area) of the room, for enhancement. This is an excellent area to hang diplomas, awards & trophies. Try to keep this area hidden from the bed.

Children's happiness and sleep patterns can be altered when in a negative location. We all have our favorite chair, room and things. Troubled, unhappy children are usually situated facing the wrong way when sleeping, eating or studying. Everyone has four prosperous, healthy directions to face... based on your pa kua energy charts while the remaining four are negative.

Growing years: Children's rooms that have electronics, are known to drain away positive energy and should be turned off, covered at night or removed. These items can leave a child lethargic and feeling tired during the day. Even if they are unplugged, this can help their health as well as the environment.

Babies require a healthy location with their head facing their best direction for peaceful, harmonized flow of energy. A restless child toss and turns trying to relocate themselves into a positive energy field.

Over stimulated children are a consequence of lack of calm and a poor diet. To increase focus, calm the space, create storage that is easy for them to utilize and better productivity and marks will be noted.

Reminder that all closets need to be de-cluttered regularly. The rule - if any item is not used in a five-month period, remove it, as its *neglect* weakens the positive energy.

Positive energy comes from having all closet hangers in the closets match in color. It is best to have them color-coded to the persons birth year energy element (wood – green; metal would be white/grey or use an actual metal material, etc.)

Bedroom locations over garages may cause 'restlessness and constant small problems' for the occupants due to poor sleep. This location is suited for a guest room, (not the Master bedroom) where there is less use.

Closet cleanse if an item has not been used, worn in the past 5-6 months, remove it; if an item has not been used in a year – get rid of it. Move on, and stop holding onto the past.

Drawers: Clean out regularly, so only positive energy enters and leaves when they are used. Messy lingerie drawers could follow you with negative energy all day, reducing clarity.

Positive energy is enhanced by having everything contained in the closets (on shelves/in boxes-baskets etc) Nothing lying 'loose'. Stay in control of your life.

Relationship problems need correction in the bedroom in the 'earth' energy area, which has become out of balance. Look in the northeast and southwest areas for clues and clutter.

No junk rooms allowed. Spend good money on storage. Difficulties arise from this if located in the north sector, trouble in the career area will appear. Junk energy in the northwest could affect friendships and travel.

Stress free buildings are those that are occupied with only things that are used, loved and needed. The rest of the items must go. Make room for wealth to grow.

Refuse to multi-task, reduce the drama and improve your health by allowing the energy to calm within and around you. Keep focused. Your inner energy will release creative ideas through inspired intuition for your needed questions.

Inspiration comes during sleep or rest periods. Bedrooms need balance yin/yang harmonized energy. Remove all stimulating items... electronics, mirrors, bright colors so that 'good' energy reaches you when sleeping.

Couples sleeping together need the head of the bed facing the direction of the 'bill payers' best direction.

The correct 'side' of the bed for sleeping is decided on the 'location' of the home carer to choose for sleeping position. (example: the man is '*west*' person so the head of the bed faces NW and the wife is an '*east*' person so she sleeps on the right side, north) Everyone benefits.

Spiritual: Love and clothe your body well, and clarity forms from the positive energy of early morning nurturing.

Align your wardrobe by color. (all whites together; blue tones; red tones etc) These color blocks keep the harmony and balance with nature – it is calming to view. Less chaotic.

Activate positive energy with music, candles, ringing of bells, waving of flags (movement) anything that makes you smile or laugh out loud.

Drenching pillows in the sun can reduce pain and headaches and produce natural and powerful healing heat.

***

Compatible Relationships

In 2003, I visited Hong Kong, a city filled with Feng Shui alignment in its architecture, gardens and roadways. I was soul-searching for a unique zodiac calendar; one with references suitable to a North American culture. This had been an ongoing search for many years and it wasn't until I made this particular trip that I found the perfect one with the right explanations.

While Hong Kong's nighttime brilliance reflects onto its harbor waters with its high energy, towering the skyline and colorful signage, it was devastating to see, as a North American, the daytime view of so many bamboo scaffoldings. At high-rise construction sites, hundreds of employees worked without proper hard hats, boots, supports or tools. The sight of them appearing to dangle over the busy streets below astounded me. It was common to hear of deaths every week during the boom construction years, and no wonder; a city without proper building codes fills with negative energy.

Following a short boat trip to Macao, I observed a magnificent example of mixed Portuguese and Chinese heritage. This mystical yet eerie island was where I located the zodiac calendar that I had been seeking. While strolling in Cathedral Square, it seemed to jump off the shelves of a rumpled old bookshop. The faded sheets of the unused tablemats described each animal of the zodiac with the appropriate characteristics. I had read many books over the years, yet I could never find the correct wording, until that moment when I knew this one was right.

My workshops and seminars include this same zodiac calendar and I owe their success to its accuracy. Clients have judged and made their comments saying it was 80-95% correct, and I think that is very good fun schway!

***

FENG SHUI ZODIAC ANIMALS

Zodiac Animal Years

1. Ox
2. Tiger
3. Rabbit
4. Dragon
5. Snake
6. Horse
7. Goat, Sheep
8. Monkey
9. Rooster, Cock
10. Dog
11. Pig, boar
12. Rat

Your birth year dictates your Zodiac Animal.

Take the 'last two numbers' of the year you were born, and minus the number 'twelve' until you reach a number less than twelve.

Match that number to the one above, and you will find your matching animal.

(e.g. 1980 would be: 80 minus 12 for 6 times (72) = 8 = Monkey)

***

The Ox

The Ox is solid and dependable.
Oxen are excellent organizers and systematic in their approach to every task they undertake.
They are not easily influenced by others' ideas.
Loyalty is part of their make-up, but if crossed or deceived they will never forget.
Oxen do not appear to be imaginative though they are capable of good ideas.
Although not demonstrative or the most exciting people romantically, they are entirely dependable and make devoted parents.
They are people of few words but fine understated gestures.
Oxen are renowned for their patience, but it has its limits – once roused, their temper is a sight to behold.

Ox is compatible with 'Snake & Rooster'

The Tiger

The Tiger is dynamic, impulsive and lives life to the full.
Tigers often leap into projects without planning, but their natural exuberance will carry them through successfully unless boredom creeps in and they do not complete the task.
Tigers do not like failure and need to be admired.
If their spirits fall, they require a patient ear to listen until they bounce back again.
They like excitement in their relationships and static situations leave them cold.
Tigers are egotistic.
They can be generous and warm, but will also sometimes show their claws.

Tigers are compatible with 'Horse & Dog'.

The Rabbit

The Rabbit is a born diplomat and cannot bear conflict.
Rabbits can be evasive and will often give the answer they think someone wishes to hear rather than enter into a discussion.
This is not to say they give in easily: the docile cover hides a strong will and self-assurance.
It is difficult to gauge what Rabbits are thinking and they can often appear to be constantly daydreaming, though in reality they may be planning their next strategy.
The calmest of the animal signs, Rabbits are social creatures up to the point when their space is invaded.
Good communication skills enable Rabbits to enjoy the company of others and they are good counselors.
They prefer to keep away from the limelight where possible and to enjoy the finer things of life.

Rabbit is compatible with 'Goat & Pig'

The Dragon

The Dragon will launch straight into projects or conversations with a pioneering spirit.
Dragons often fall to notice others trying to keep up or indeed those plotting behind their backs.
Authority figures, they make their own laws and cannot bear restriction.
They prefer to get on with a job themselves and are good at motivating others into action.
They are always available to help others, but their pride makes it difficult for them to accept help in return.
Although they are always at the centre of things, they tend to be loners and are prone to stress when life becomes difficult.
Hard working and generous, Dragons and entirely trustworthy and are loyal friends.
They enjoy excitement and new situations.
When upset, they can be explosive, but all soon forgotten.

Dragon is compatible with 'Rat & Monkey'

The Snake

The Snake is a connoisseur of the good things in life.
Inward looking and self-reliant, Snakes tend to keep their own counsel and dislike relying on others.
They can be ruthless in pursuing their goals.
Although very kind and generous, Snakes can be demanding in relationships.
They find it hard to forgive and will never forget a slight.
Never underestimate the patience of a snake, which will wait in the wings until the time is right to strike.
They are elegant and sophisticated and although they are good at making money, they never spend it on trifles.
Only the best is good enough for them.
Very intuitive, Snakes can sense the motives of others and can sum up situations accurately.
If crossed, Snakes will bite back with deadly accuracy.
They exude an air of mystery, ooze charm and can be deeply passionate.

Snake is compatible with 'Ox & Rooster'.

The Horse

The Horse is every-active.
Horses will work tirelessly until a project is completed, but only if the deadline is their own.
Horses have lightning minds and can sum up people and situations in an instant, sometimes too quickly, and they will move on before seeing the whole picture.
Capable of undertaking several tasks at once, Horses are constantly on the move and fond of exercise.
They may exhaust themselves physically and mentally.
Horses are ambitious and confident in their own abilities.
They are not interested in the opinions of others and are adept at side-stepping issues.
They can be impatient and have explosive tempers although they rarely bear grudges.

Horse is compatible with 'Tiger & Dog'

The Goat

The Goat is emotional and compassionate.
Peace-lovers, Goats always behave correctly and they are extremely accommodating to others.
They tend to be shy and vulnerable to criticism.
They worry a lot and appear to be easily put upon, but when they feel strongly about something they will dig their heels in and sulk until they achieve their objectives.
Goats are generally popular and are usually well cared for by others.
They appreciate the finer things in life and are usually lucky.
They find it difficult to deal with difficulties and deprecation.
Ardent romantics, Goats can obtain their own way by wearing their partners down and turning every occasion to their advantage.
They will do anything to avoid conflict and hate making decisions.

Goat is compatible with 'Rabbit & Pig'.

The Monkey

The Monkey is intelligent and capable of using its wits to solve problems.
Monkeys' often wriggle out of difficult situations and are not above trickery if it will further their own ends.
Monkeys tend to be oblivious of other people and of the effect their own actions may have on them.
In spite of this, they are usually popular and are able to motivate others by sheer enthusiasm for new projects.
Monkeys challenge and their innovative approach and excellent memories generally make them successful.
They are full of energy and are always active.
They have little sympathy for those who are unable to keep up with, but will soon forget any difficulties.

Monkey is compatible with 'Rat & Dragon'.

The Rooster

The Rooster is a very sociable creature.
Roosters shine in situations where they are able to be the centre of attention.
If a Rooster is present, everyone will be aware of the fact because no Rooster can ever take a back seat at a social gathering.
They are dignified, confident and extremely strong-willed, yet they may have a negative streak.
They excel in arguments and debates.
Incapable of underhandedness, Roosters lay all their cards on the table and do not spare others' feelings in their quest to do the right thing.
They never weary of finding the underlying cause of a problem and are perfectionists in all that they do.
Roosters can usually be won over by flattery. Full of energy, Roosters are brave, but they hate criticism and can be puritanical in their approach to life.

Rooster is compatible with 'Ox & Snake'.

The Dog

The Dog is entirely dependable and has an inherent sense of justice.
Intelligent, Dogs are loyal to their friends and they always listen to the problems of others, although they can be critical.
In a crisis, Dogs will always help and they will never betray a friend.
They can be hard workers, but are not very interested in accumulating wealth for themselves.
They like to spend time relaxing.
Dogs take time to get to know people but have a tendency to pigeon-hole them.
When they want something badly they can be persistent.
If roused they can be obstinate and occasionally they lash out, although their temper is usually short-lived.
Some Dogs can be rather nervous and they may be prone to pessimism.

Dog is compatible with 'Tiger & Horse'

The Pig

The Pig is everybody's friend.
Honest and generous, they are always available to bail others out of difficulties.
Pigs love the social scene and are popular.
They rarely argue and if they do fly off the handle, they bear no grudges afterwards.
They abhor conflict and very often will not notice when others are attempting to upset them.
They prefer to think well of people.
Over indulgence is their greatest weakness and Pigs will spend heavily in pursuit of pleasure.
They always share with their friends and trust that, in return, their friends with make allowances for their own little weaknesses.
Great organizers, Pigs like to have a cause and will often rally others to it as well.

Pig is compatible with 'Rabbit & Goat'.

The Rat

The Rat is an opportunist with an eye for a bargain.
Rats tend to collect and hoard, but are unwilling to pay too much for anything.
They are devoted to their families, particularly their children.
On the surface, Rats are sociable and gregarious yet underneath they can be miserly and petty.
Quick-witted and passionate, they are capable of deep emotions despite their cool exteriors.
Their nervous energy and ambition may lead Rats to attempt more tasks than they can able to complete successfully.

Rat is compatible with 'Dragon & Monkey'

(Six)
KNOWLEDGE

Command the forces of nature.
Feel the sun and believe,
Feel the earth and be relieved,
Touch the water and receive
The energy breath of the wind
and feel free.

***

Ch'i movement of energy warns of clogged & filled drains that must be kept clear for easy water flow, which helps to keep the lives of those in the building healthy.

Storage spaces should be closed rather than left open, so as not to attract energy-flow away from the prosperous meandering path.

Wet rooms carry negative energy - bathrooms with toilets, open drains; kitchen & garbage; laundry and dirt. These areas should be located in the occupants *'worst 4 locations'* of the building based on their personal pa kua charts.

Positive energy can be encouraged by keeping the drains plugged; toilet seats down at all times to prevent any financial energy from going down the drain especially if these rooms are located in the 'wealth' area of the building, which would be in the southeast location.

Negative energy from bathroom and kitchen odors can be corrected naturally with a vase of fresh flowers.

"Wet rooms" should *not* be stimulated or activated with 'enhancements' or other remedies in the "Wealth or Relationship" areas because this will only draw more energies that are negative.

***

University Lifestyle

University towns and cities that overflow with students provide a few places with a vibrant 'pub' life. Many graduates love to study on the west coast for several reasons, and if their schooling happened to fit into their social life, all the better. From California to British Columbia, University towns are places for fun for the outdoor type of students and their active lifestyle.

Mark Winslow from Detroit, Michigan and Marcia Lefebvre from Montreal were spending an afternoon at the Royal British Museum. They were in a line-up for tickets to view the Imax showing of a Rock Concert. I was amongst many 'under 30 groups' waiting for the doors to open to the theatre. The couple was in line behind me, chatting about the great city they had discovered, being Victoria. We loved hearing this, especially from those younger than seventy. We had a brief conversation, advising them on some fun spots to visit. It was early December and Marcia explained that she wasn't looking forward to going back to Quebec for Christmas. She was enjoying the Mediterranean climate. They lived in an apartment near U-Vic campus and could walk to classes.

The line-up into the theatre had begun to move when Mark explained his Engineering studies were giving him some difficulties. They were more than he bargained for, and something else was bothering him about their place.

There was a commotion in the back of the line. We turned to see a broken escalator had caused havoc as fifty or sixty people began stammering, making their way around the corner to find stairs. I commented. 'Yuck. Negative energy!' The couple laughed.

'What's that all about?' they inquired with an inquisitive grin. We started to move forward, again, as I explained it wasn't great to be around things damaged, cracked or broken as this stagnates the surrounding positive energy.

"And... with all those people complaining, it doesn't help make things better'.

Marcia turned to Mark. "That must be it, Mark. Your study room has a broken window, burnt out light and God knows what all." She laughed.

As we entered into the theatre, I said, "Don't laugh! It's true."

The Mick Jagger concert turned out to be fabulous; a great show that everyone enjoyed. When it finished, a few of us proceeded across the road to the Spaghetti Factory to get a bite to eat.

Upon departing the restaurant, we walked to our parked vehicles. The young couple we had encountered in the lineup earlier that evening approached me. Mark was surprised that we had run into each other again as they had just been talking about me. He had wanted to know if I knew of anyone who might help with the set up of their apartment in regards to our earlier conversation. I quickly retrieved a business card, and offered my services.

First thing, in the New Year, I visited their apartment. It was a good size compared to all the new towers that were being constructed in the city. Their apartment was built in the late 70's; it was due for a renovation.

I found their corner unit bright, which gave the overall atmosphere a good feeling. A couple of large windows allowed light into the unit, but I felt something that bothered me. There was a strong sense of negative energy about the place, a hurtful feeling.

Marcia offered Mark and me a cup of green tea as we walked through the unit. He kept pretty quiet about it all, while Marcia chatted as to the lack of storage. They had a lot of 'stuff' for two students. Finally, I turned to Mark to hear his comments.

Apparently, he never felt comfortable in the suite. He found his studies harder than expected, and just felt kind of 'down' most of the time. I entered the room where he studied finding a lot of stuff from computers, drafting boards, books upon books stacked around the space. In addition, the room had a badly cracked window.

I didn't like the fact that he sat with his back to the door when sitting at his computer. After a few minutes, I suggested a new way to realign his studies, as I wanted him situated in the

'Knowledge' sector of the room, which was near the window where he would receive good light. I recommended IKEA for some needed storage shelves, and to get some of the backpacks, and boxes into storage. We organized the space as I explained they needed to have the window covered with something. A light sheer fabric would *not* reduce the light into the room, but would cover the damage until their landlord could get the window repaired.

We returned to the dark hallway filled with numerous scattered pairs of shoes. They needed to place them on a mat or on a shelf in the limited space, which would retain the negative energy that they brought into the unit from the outside. Often, shoes were not allowed into the home because of the dirty areas they had walked through. Heaven only knows what you might bring into the home from the bottom of your shoes. To stay in control of this *sha ch'i*, place all shoes onto a mat or shelf.

Feeling something hurtful about this space, as if the walls were vibrating with the need to be cared for, I understood Mark's uneasy feeling about the suite. (Your most powerful instinct is 'feeling' the energy.)

We moved into the kitchen next. Not great, so to speak. The cupboards had several broken handles, cracked tile on the floor, and badly soiled and damaged counter tops. This space was totally negative. I requested the whole room cleared out. We began from scratch and making a list of things to purchase, some new dishes, and get rid of all the chipped and mismatched items. Wal-Mart was fine for making these purchases. I didn't care where, or what they selected, they just needed to get some stability into the 'nurturing' space. Everything required cleaning, and repairs completed, so it was time to call the Landlord for some assistance.

The old cupboards needed washing as well as all the windows and windowsills. A floor mat by the sink covered the cracked tile, until the landlord could attend to repairing it, and a candle was lit while they cleansed. The view from the window was nothing more than the rooftop of the next-door building and had to be camouflaged with some kind of covering. The things they could not change, like the stove (Fire element) was situated across from the refrigerator (Water element) and sink - an area of huge negative energy, as Water drowns Fire. The energy of earth was needed to reduce the water-energy, so a square or rectangle mat was recommended between the two. As long as they were aware of this, things would be better. It's never a good idea or recommended to eat in the kitchen working-area because of its state and they would find it much healthier eating elsewhere. Arguments and mishaps follow bad energy.

We took a break in the living area of the apartment. I asked Mark about his thoughts regarding the place. He explained that they didn't have a lot of choices when it was time to find a place to live when they moved in, as school was only a couple of weeks from starting and they were on a budget. He said that he just never felt comfortable living there.

I asked them to play detective and find out about the previous tenants. It might be interesting to hear why they moved out.

I left them with a list of several things to move, clean and beware of. Recommending they ask the landlord either to paint the unit or offer to do it if he paid for the paint, I left the color chips and listed the proper finishes to use.

By mid February, Mark called my Studio. He wanted me to drop by their apartment. He explained that he had done some research and found out that the last tenants had lived there for ten months. They were a group of 4 students crammed into the space. The tenants before them were an elderly couple that had lived there for over 20 years. The alcoholic husband was very abusive. According to other tenants in the building, there fought a lot and a couple of times, the ambulance had to come to the unit. Finally, he suffered a stroke and placed into a recovery unit, and the wife moved back east to live with her family.

I explained to Marcia and Mark that the space lacked attention, and all the incoming energy turned negative. The hostile vibration was what Mark had sensed from the beginning of their stay. The environment lacked harmony and had no sense of well-being. He felt his studies were suffering because of it.

When I returned to the apartment, they had it filled with flowers. The old furniture they collected was situated on angles and was color co-ordinated with matching accessories, pillows and throws, which was just the right amount, not overfilling the room. Every inch of space was tended-to, painted and fixed up. Greenery filled corners in wicker containers and a sense of love filled their apartment.

The windows covered with tab-top, floor-length textured sheers, so not to hinder the incoming light but hid the view. The older kitchen sparkled, and all the repairs were completed with nothing left out on the countertops. Even the knives, considered weapons, were tucked away behind a cupboard door. Their new color scheme of ivory, white and grey-green was soothing.

Mark was the first to comment that he actually felt good about his courses, and that his marks were improving. The nurtured space became positive, no longer abused, as they completed each task with special care and a little help from the landlord.

If you don't love your home, don't stay there.
Never stay in someone else's negative energy. It only weakens your own good fortune. Be knowledgeable about how it feels.

A building is also a living structure, vibrating with its own energy created by all those that built and worked on it, as well as those who had lived in it. Create your own harmony and prosper.

Good fun schway... says Grannie!

***

The *Kitchen* is the room that nurtures you the most, but carries both positive and negative energies.

Kitchens represent 'nourishment' extending health & wealth. All the preparation surfaces should be cleaned with lemon & water solutions and stay clear of clutter so not to weaken any 'abundance' from the occupants. This space carries negative energy from the burning fire (hot stove) dirty prep (washing dishes) spills, soils and harshness that goes into preparing foods.

The room should be free from harmful chemicals, so not to weaken the 'health' of the occupants.

Well-stocked cupboards with fresh food items create abundance. Toss out anything not consumed or used to open space up for new... abundance... not holding on to negative past energies from stale foods, seasonings and foods past their expiry dates on boxes and can products.

After checking expiry dates, dispose all overdue items.

Yin/Yang in the kitchen is accomplished by incorporating all the elements (5) by material, color or shape.

White cabinets would represent 'metal-energy'
Stove/oven would represent 'fire-energy'
Tile floor would represent 'earth-energy'
Sink/dishwasher would represent 'water-energy'
Greenery or wallpaper would represent 'wood-energy'.

Feng Shui warning that mirrors in the kitchen only encourages more fire; water etc which would be damaging to the energy 'balance' of the space.

Kitchen Islands should contain an 'earth' element when situated in the centre of the room. Example would be granite, tile, marble or a concrete surface. These surfaces should remain clear when not in use. The soul of the room.

Excess Yin in a room can be altered with natural sunlight, electric lights or windows which can be effectively used to expel the excessive yin (dark corners) creating a more balanced space.

Hide all weapons when not in use. (Knives, toasters, blenders or anything else that changes the consistency, shape or temperature of the food.)

Health is weakened when the occupants eat in the kitchen 'working area' or in any wet room as this can add to poor health issues.

Kitchens operate best when *not* located beneath other 'wet rooms' where negative energies are found to be 'pressing down' on it. (i.e. bathroom)

Calming the kitchen can be done by color co-ordinating counter tops & back splashes with same color; blending in the appliances (so not to be easily identified) with cabinet fronts... all to help reduce visual clutter.

Kitchen & Bathroom 'windows' are fire elements and must be kept clear and clean to encourage good health and prevent negative energy from entering. Nothing on the window-sills.

Too much fire-energy in the kitchen is not good... reduce the color red, excess lighting (not used) too many windows, stoves near a window, exposed grills, toasters, kettles, diamond or cone shapes. These can trigger arguments, mishaps and damage relationships.

High tech kitchens are designed for the gourmet cook; but if you live on fast foods, take-outs or small meals, opt for the *juicer* for vegetables and a sandwich grill instead, enhancing your finances for other luxuries.

Harshness:
Don't cleanse a space with harsh chemicals that will kill off its positive energy; use natural products if possible, to reflect a caring, healthy home. Clean-up with detergent, lime and vinegar solutions.

Wet rooms should be well lit (even if on dimmer switches) and good under-cabinet lighting highlights food prep areas.

Kitchen calming can be positive when playing joyful, fun music to change the mood of the task when cooking or cleaning.

Feng Shui warns to orientate the 'mouth' of the oven to the 'owners best direction' (breadwinner) and *not* point out the kitchen door.

Kitchens items stored, but rarely used should be removed from the space, so as *not* to stagnate the energy. Keep cabinets filled with only 'used' items and free from overcrowding that causes confusion and poor memory.

Never cook/warm food in any type of *plastic containers* in the microwave. Poison to your health. Microwaves are not recommended, or anything plastic around food. Put into glass containers to protect against growing diseases.

Nurturing kitchens are those that have no complications. Clean appliances and a well-equipped room without malfunctioning items all help prevent agitation and anxiety around the home.

Harmful 'health' energy comes from off-gassing plastics that contain foods. Replace items into glass (earth) containers or other natural elements to prevent unnecessary illness. Containers made of plastic (water bottles) are especially bad for water if ever left in the sun for any length of time.

Energy flow can be enhanced by NOT having a <u>water</u> element (fridge) situated opposite a <u>fire</u> element (stove) so not to drown its prosperous energies, bringing unnecessary hardships and conflicting opinions.

Bathrooms: locate them 'away' from the front entry for safety as well as protecting the incoming positive energy. Loss of good energy 'down-the-drain' and weakening of incoming friendships can be avoided.

Mirrors should never reflect the toilet... only to double the draining effect of positive energy.

Bathroom negatives are from toilets situated directly facing the entry door that only encourages the negative energies to spread throughout the building.

Bathrooms and its negative energy should be kept separate from other areas with solid sound-proofing insulated walls constructed from concrete board or similar products.

Orderly bathrooms are ones with 'just the necessary' toiletries that are used. Get rid of the rest and check the expiry dates of medicines regularly.

Never leave damp towels on the floor as it sucks up all the enhancing 'luck' energy of the home.

***

NOTES:

(Seven)
ATTRACTION

When searching for new ways to enrich your life,
be open to ideas that come to you through
mysterious means and uncharted paths,
from the unexpected mystical
movement of energy.

***

Aspirations for the Workplace.
The 'wealth' area is the southeast sector and a good place in the building for an office. Client files within the sector enhance the space but not good area for bills, debts and negative literature.

Along with an 'activation remedy' to enhance the energy of the Career sector, this would be accomplished by placing a water element 'fountain' or 'fish tank' next to a flowering plant in a brass planter pot in north or the southeast. A number of Asian restaurants will have such a remedy at their entrance door.

Clutter in the Wealth Sector can enhance negative energy, adding unnecessary debt and unwanted anxiety. Enclose all papers out-of-sight so not to expose to doubling the debt.

Wealth Sector (Southeast)
can be diminished when white walls or white cabinets dominate the space; the energy flow becomes 'still' from any growth because 'white' is the color for 'metal-energy' which controls/cuts wood which is the element for southeast.

Work attitudes affect your mood and this energy carries with you into other areas of your life. If you don't love your work, make changes... as it will make a difference to your environment and your relationships.

Business Intentions are written and placed in your daytimer for new goals, and successes to be reached.

***

Financial Loss Reversed

One Saturday morning, I ventured into the studio to catch up on last minute prep work for an upcoming seminar - 'Color Energy in the Workplace'. I had just closed down the computer files, counted the required portfolios needed for the attendees and was about to lock up.

Loud stomping footsteps sounded on the staircase leading up to my studio located on the second floor. A knock pushed the door ajar and in stepped two middle-aged men, sporting Levi's and leather jackets, with one carrying a large tan envelope. I recognized the shorter of the two. It was Ron Coleman, an artist I had previously worked with in Toronto. I heard he had moved to the Portland area a few years back, but we had lost contact.

We introduced ourselves once again. His cousin, Stew, was acting as chauffeur for him, being a native to the Victoria area. We chatted for a bit, catching up on each other's whereabouts and happenings. Both men were familiar with my work in the energy field and Ron had consulted with me before on planning his premises for his personal art shows. He was an accomplished artist and knowledgeable, as I remembered, about Classic Feng Shui applications, and had been prosperous in all his endeavors

Ron understood the concepts of enhancing the Career Sector of his building before any art showing. He was aware of the importance of energy flow into his space and the need to make sure positive energy complemented his personal Feng Shui charts. Even though he knew what to do, he said something was amiss. His dilemma was that he was broke and just couldn't get things right anymore. It didn't matter what he tried he couldn't change the flow. When I assisted Ron before, he had been working in pastels, charcoals and some oils. His pieces were both peaceful while others were energized, showing a unique talent to attract a varied market of purchasers. He changed mediums and was now working in stone, sculptures and marble.

Stew pulled open his envelope and showed me several newspaper articles describing Ron's 'exquisite' pieces and lengthy columns praising his technique and creative images. Both puzzled over this as the media accepted Ron's work; but nothing sold at his showings.

I explained that I no longer had any of his personal files and needed to have his Energy charts calculated before I could view his workplace. He was planning a three-week showing beginning the following week. I told him I would do my best to get back to him no later than Tuesday when we would meet again. I wrote down all the information I needed, and we left it at that.

The following week, Ron's Charts were ready. We met for a Decaf at Mocha House in Cook Street Village and went over his charts. I could see he agreed with them all, but he couldn't identify any missing items or situations while preparing for his show.

I learned that Ron worked in his new art form for just over a year. It was about that time when his finances began to diminish. We headed to his location.

He parked his van across the street from his building. The address was 2921... not bad; for his charts indicated he was a *'West'* energy person and the number 2 was prosperous and all the numbers totaled 5 which again was good for a *West* male. The energy flow into his building was northeast direction (which also was just fine); therefore indicating that the structure 'sits' southwest which also was perfect. The studio was located on the second floor. The building was old and not as bright as I would have liked it to be, but it was painted well, no chips or damage and in relatively good care.

Ron unlocked the door to his studio. The key worked smoothly, nothing sticking. He entered; I waited for a few seconds. I placed the compass at the entry. His space had an entry direction of west (good) but meant that his space would 'sit' east... not great, as it would be classified as an *East* location for him. However, it did have fabulous light within the interior for his work from the windows. I spent a few minutes feeling out my 'first impression'. The entry opened into the very large room. Something didn't feel just right.

Ron carried energy from his birth year (Yang Water). There was some walls painted charcoal on the east, and ivory on the north, which were both 'enhancing' colors to the building's aspirations.

Numerous spot-lites highlighted his work; it appeared dramatic but also Zen-like with just the right amount of greenery in south to enhance his personal 'recognition'.

The large counter space for work, laptop etc was located in the Wealth sector of the room (southeast=wood) It was well lit, and he would face northwest when sitting... which was good. The space was well organized, and clean. A beautiful healthy violet plant situated on the corner of his work desk.

Ron's creative workspace was constructed from wood, which was correct for this southeast sector, and his chair was covered in a woven fabric carrying all the colors of the elements in a small wave-like pattern. A large, framed, watercolor (Ron painted) of the mountains in Whistler Village was situated behind the desk, providing him with good support.

The area for his carving of sculptures was located in his prosperous location, west side of the room. At first, I thought his back might be facing the entry door, but realized he had set it up correctly. He walked around throwing up his arms in disgust... just not getting it. He thought the space should be more prosperous. The old brick walls and wood floor added some character, but did not show any damage from neglect. They were just aged. The energy flow in the space was meandering and without conflict. All Ron's art, sculptures were displayed in the north (career sector) of the room. He had always displayed his art in this sector. This was great when he was painting.

Unexpectedly, I laughed aloud and threw up my arms as I pointed to the display area. He shook his head, not understanding. I pointed directly, again. He shook his head again, pondering the matter. I walked over to his display area. The north sector carries water-energy in the Career sector. North sector is *Career* everywhere, in every building, every city, and in every room. He knows that. However, now his art form was consistently an earth element (stone). I picked up an item admiring its beauty and precise detailing. Exquisite!

I said... "Ron. Earth dominates (dams) water. Earth 'controls' and weakens water-energy and therefore will totally reduce the positive energy in this area. It weakens, destroys the energy of the Career sector making it negative. This area or location is perfect for your paintings on canvas or paper... but these new creations need to be located in a sector holding the energy of 'earth' which would be northeast sector or southwest sector of the room to attract positive energy."

Ron threw up his arms... but this time, smiling, understanding the theory. "I knew that," he said. I explained that he was a Yang Water person. He was working with an earth element (stone) that was only attracting negative energy into his life. The negative changes had nothing to do with his talent. He had correctly placed 'his work' in the Career sector, which was water element, and therefore the Career sector of the studio became weakened. He was totally amazed that he had missed the whole cycle of *Element Enhancement & Control Theory*. We both laughed heartily as we realized the walls of his space consisted mostly of brick, another earth element that resonated negative energy around him. He was just inundated with being and working in the wrong energy field and never caught on to it.

Another look at his space, and we decided to make corrections. The walls would be painted in a suede finish, silver grey, leaving the texture of the brick showing, but it would reduce the energy from earth to metal (color) which is the *enhancement element* for Ron. He installed numerous black platforms, shelving and displays for his items, to bring Water (color black) into his space; relocated his showroom display area for his sculptures to the southwest sector. We added splashes of red to the south sector (to promote his '*recognition*') with bouquets of red flowers and cushions for his black leather sofa and we framed several newspaper clippings about his successes, in black frames. I encouraged Ron to rethink his medium – as the sculptures were beautiful, but truly, not the best product for 'abundance' and creating positive energy for him in that studio.

Sometimes, it is difficult to see what's right in front of our eyes; and need to step aside and view our environment, listen to our intuition, and then create a balanced space filled with positive energy. Ron succeeded at his opening art show where he sold over $45,000.00!

Good fun schway... says Grannie!

Success:
Crystals only 'enhance' when placed in southwest or northeast locations! Keep their energy prosperous in the west energy field. Nurture them by cleaning them regularly, keeping them active by resting in the sun.

Success can be encouraged by placing a group of 'red' candles on a wood or green tray and locate it in the south sector of a south room. Always burn the tips beforehand so they do not appear unused or neglected.

Lingbi stones (earth) carry stronger energy when placed near candles or lamps (fire) in these NE, W, NW or SW sectors of a room to enhance ones creativity, awareness, friendships and knowledge.

Feng Shui recommends placing any personal recognition on the south wall area. Example would be diplomas, trophies, awards, media print, photos, etc.

Support yourself with a 'high back' chair or solid wall behind the back of the chair when working, paying bills or being creative.

Powerful art such as mountains or towering buildings all provide strength & always protect your back in a workplace or study area.

The desk represents income, prosperity and creative energies. Organize all papers and 'contain' them so they don't appear scattered: bills-invoices keep out of sight so not to draw additional debt.

Feng Shui warns to keep the energy positive, by removing all cracked, damaged or broken items... even pens and pencils... so not to cause hardships.

De-clutter to dispose ALL non-essential papers for a clearer vision: 'out of sight – out of mind!'

Subconscious energy drainer is clutter, an unorganized space. Eliminate unnecessary files for clarity and a new awareness opens up. Leave ten percent empty space for *new* to enter.

Fire element: The desk and any work surfaces should have the 'fire-energy' (enhancement) present by being well lit. Good light from windows or lamps represents this element and clarity.

Water elements should <u>not</u> be placed behind your desk, including mirrors. Change any artwork if there are rivers, lakes, or predominantly black colors in it.

Energy flow
An office needs maneuvering ability for better creativity, thought and memory. Analyze the space carefully.

Fresh flowers in the office near or on the desk attract growth when cared for regularly.

Your work:
Write your intention and keep it somewhere close by, such as establishing a place of wellbeing and abundance, and your goals.

Interior items need to be moved, touched when cleaning so the whole space has been activated with positive energy and your mood must also be 'up.' Break routine.

Bad luck in the Career area can be altered by placing two round stones in the north area of your desk to dissolve or change it. (Earth controls water). Remove them once things change.

Trouble in the Creativity sector (west) can be altered by placing red candles in this space until the energy breaks and turns positive.

Bad working relationships could alter with a dose of 'flowering plants' placed in the southwest sector.

Recognition: successes you have accomplished should be visually clear and located in the <u>south</u> sector. Any 'good' your profession has attained, business accomplishments and testimonials should always be available for others to see.

Don't locate your desk under a window (fire element) unless the window has some sort of covering. Too much fire could lead to distractions, burnout or lack of focus.

Be specific when selecting furniture. Too many wood elements are not suitable furniture for those born in an 'earth' energy year, so not to feel overworked and getting nowhere.

Beware of sharp corners: watch that there are no poison arrows (protruding corners) facing or hitting you or your back when working so not to experience anxiety, misfortunes, headaches or, defective electronics.

***

NOTES:

Negative Business Discussions

Competition in business can be a stressful venture. One particular incident comes to mind.

In the fall of a very wet, rainy season in Toronto, I just returned from Chicago and was in the midst of finalizing an installation to a Corporate Headquarters lobby in the Don Mills area. Everything was near completion. The granite flooring, topped with colorful Tufenkian carpets, was cleaned for loose threads; the walls were covered in silk fabric-backed material and the windows were topped with the latest Hunter Douglas product. The custom furniture was being placed as the artwork was installed when I called a halt... 'Whoops! Not there, Edward... that's not great Feng Shui." He rolled his eyes, smiling

I felt an unexpected tap on my left shoulder from behind. Startled at first, I quickly turned only to gasp at the sight of the company's CEO smiling down at me. 'Oh, no!' I thought to myself. 'He doesn't like it.'

The scene stopped from a hectic rush to silence. No one moved. He introduced himself, and then invited me to follow him to his corporate office. No one made a sound as I shadowed the man down what seemed a never-ending hallway to a private elevator. Within minutes, we entered a space that vibrated with the energy of grandeur. He offered me a seat in one of the cream leather sofas, which centered on a window with a view overlooking the colorful valley.

A silver tray sat on a black onyx table in front of me, holding a large Waterford crystal water pitcher that he grasped and poured two glasses of the sparkling liquid. He sat opposite me explaining that he heard my comment about Feng Shui, in the lobby. The CEO described how he knew very little about the subject other than what he heard about during his travels abroad. He wanted to know more.

A strong sense of relief settled over my whole being, relieved to know that our meeting had nothing to do with the design of the new lobby. I cleared by throat as if I had some congestion when it was only a nervous reaction.

I explained the concept of the mystical movement of energy and its effect on the environment as well as our personal well-being. He listened attentively and had many questions.

His concern was that his Tech Company that had numerous dealings with Asian countries was losing a number of contracts. He wondered if Feng Shui realignment could have anything to do with changing things for his company. I thought his inquiry was because of a substantial decrease in sales. We spent some time discussing many of his different business dealings.

The 6'2" man stood up and paced the office momentarily while rubbing his hands through his thick graying hair. He explained that most of the company's business dealings took place in the building that we were in and that everyone concerned in preparing each contract would gather to discuss the details, product lines, deliveries, availabilities of the items negotiated. I suggested we look at the room where these meetings took place. I wanted to know who and how many would be at a meeting.

He explained their usual procedure. Typically, three visiting people and two or three representatives, executives or managers from different departments would attend, depending on the situation.

When we entered the room, my first impression was that of stagnant energy. I felt the rectangle table needed to be turned the opposite direction and would have been better if it was an oval shape. He glanced around the room observing my comments that the space lacked a Life element, as there was no greenery, which limited growth. This would help with the air quality control of the off-gassing of the synthetic carpeting in the enclosed space. I listed a few large, round leaf plants, for the southeast sector to enhance the finance area, in matching decorative ceramic pots. In addition, the large floor to ceiling windows that covered two walls represented a sign of vulnerability when not covered.

I excused myself to return to the lobby to retrieve my briefcase and my compass. The four decorators rushed to my side to find out what was happening. I explained that it had nothing to do with our design work. I sensed an air of relief from all as I quickly made my way back to the company's boardroom.

Taking a second view of the space didn't seem to enlighten me any. The room was located in the northeast section, which is the Knowledge sector of the building. This was an excellent space for discussions. (It could also do well in the northwest sector, a people and friendship sector.) The room needed an energy boost. I suggested a large red-tone earth element on the centre of the table. I recommended adding an item that he felt attracted to... a sculpture, bowl, or flowers, whatever he fancied, but suggested an earth element to keep things grounded.

The space just didn't feel prosperous. We discussed the history of the company, which had been very successful, and suggested a large photo of the company, or some kind of archive to do with its past on the west wall, enhancing the Creativity of the business.

I learned that a typical meeting would last four or five hours depending on the size of the contract. Describing the importance of having his people sit at the table in their *Best Energy* field, they should face one of their four best directions.

Detailing the facts, that every person has specific Energy Charts calculated from their birth year revealing their positive and negative locations - most Eastern or Asian individuals are aware of this factor and intuitively know where to sit. They automatically place themselves at a table in their most powerful energy field. The meetings that had taken place were conducted in such a matter, that the guests were directed to the boardroom and allowed to enter and sit themselves first, followed by his company's executives. I suggested breaking this pattern. The CEO reached for a pen from his jackets inside pocket and jotted a few notes down as I spoke.

At our next meeting, I recommended that his people allow their guests to enter as usual to have their discussions; but clear the table and break the meeting for lunch. On their return to the boardroom, have his employees enter the room first, and sit down where the guests had previously sat, making sure that his executives were located in one their own positive energy fields. By doing this, it would break the energy flow, and confuse his guests, briefly. Whenever there's change within a room, it confuses the flow of energy, and a definite shift takes place as the electromagnetic field affects each one differently. It's a fact of life. It's no different from when you attend a gathering and sit down in a comfortable place, but then leave your seat briefly. When you return, someone else has sat there. There's a moment of confusion, a shift in attitude, confusion etc until you settle.

We discussed the process further, and then I returned to the lobby to finish the design for the final touches to the décor.

A few days later, I heard back from the company with the birthdates of three managers that would be in discussions with a potential new client. I completed their personal Energy charts and met with each one individually for an overview, and then we all got together the day before the meeting to detail the plan and explain how the process worked. The meeting would be with a firm from Tokyo and if the new client bought the Tech companies proposal, it would be a deal worth millions of dollars.

Each Executive knew exactly his or her 'best location' to sit in the boardroom when their meeting would stop for lunch, and they would return to complete negotiations. No one was to sit with their back to the entry door or face a protruding corner of a wall (pointed edge) known as a poison arrow, as this alters the energy flow; (its sharpness cuts the air, causing negative energy.) The room was enhanced with natural elements and brighter upholstery on the chair coverings to incorporate all colors of all the five elements to make sure there would be no lack. The large window-walls had a control element installed, (screen-rollerblinds) for protection, which didn't block out the light. They just controlled it. Change the flow of energy and change your results.

The meeting took place and the Tokyo visitors entered the boardroom first with their coffees and portfolios, seated themselves and began discussions. The company's executives and managers noted their placements. The day went as planned. The meeting resumed after their lunch break with the executives seating themselves first in their new positions, placing their files down where their guests had previously sat and situated themselves to face one of their best directions taking in positive energy.

With the shift in energy, their guests were confused at first, as we all are when we return to our seat to find it occupied. Things feel out of balance. The company's executives resumed their negotiations in a new, compelling manner.

The success of positioning the body in its correct energy field comes with good intuition and awareness. Even if you are losing an argument, move around. This forces the other person to shift positions, breaking the energy pattern. Because of this new understanding, I was rewarded well, and assisted the company several times, receiving large bouquets of flowers from the CEO for many years.

Good fun schway... says Grannie!

(Eight)
SPACE CLEANSING

Look closely around your building's exterior and interior.
Pay close attention to your inner thoughts.

Don't bring your past to the present
because it will dominate your future.

***

Why Cleanse?

Background:
Throughout the 1980s and 1990s, the North American population was exposed to large numbers of new technologies, new toys, new home decorating products and more disposable income. The 'uncluttered home' of the past became filled with 'things'. The more 'things', the more off-gassing from products, which caused the depletion of natural resources-elements. Eventually, less spare time became available to organize these possessions resulting in a cluttered, unhealthy environment, which causes poor health.

This new millennium demands new ways of looking at this issue and overcoming the complaints of the day... headaches, stress, disorder, feeling drained and tired. When products in the office and home produce ill effects, it is time to analyze your surroundings and be aware of changes.

EMF (electromagnetic fields), both positive and negative energies, flow freely in a healthy and prosperous environment. It is all about seeking balance and keeping it.

Purpose of space cleansing:

- To make healthy corrections to our surroundings, which affect our career, wealth, creativity, health and relationships.
- To enhance your home and office with a sense of overall wellbeing and prosperity.
- To produce a feeling of continuity and balance.
- To create a space where you are productive.
- To remove negative energy and fill the space with universal positive energy.
- To create 'environmentally friendly interiors'.

When to space cleanse.

Positive energy (chi) should gently circulate around the room like a meandering stream. Too much clutter changes the flow of healthy chi energy into negative 'sha chi' energy.

As 'needless' things are released and removed, (just like unwanted burdens, the load gets lighter) a new clarity is realized... an energized space. If there is no space for the 'new' to come into your life then the 'old' dominates and accumulates until an unhealthy environment develops.

The time to space cleanse is when you need 'correction' in the areas of Career, Health, Relationships, Creativity and Wealth.

The cleansing process revitalizes you and the space.

How to Space Cleanse.

Get a pencil and answer the following (honestly).

Are your closets overfilled? With what?

Is there 'stuff' behind doors? What kind of stuff? Why?

Are there boxes and things that haven't been used in several months? What's in them? How long have they been there?

Are there any shoes and things lying around the floors? Where? How many and why?

Anything stored under the bed? What? For how long?

Any clutter in the corners? What is it and why?

Any uncovered laundry baskets or trash cans? Where? (It could be in your romance area.)

Loose papers scattered on tables, floors or furniture? Why?

Any 'things around you that you don't need, use or love? Why?

Are ALL surfaces 50% clear of 'things'?

Anything cracked, damaged or broken? What and where are they?

Are there any stale aromas?

Procedure:

Select a closet first.
Always record your answers.
Before starting, state your first impression.

How does it make you feel?

Play music. (Sound is required at 'space cleansing' time and it should be something that inspires you. music you love.

Keep a record of what music you played.

***

Prepare a Space Cleansing Kit of your own.

You need all the natural elements in your presence (sample idea)

Fire - candle
Metal - plate, coins or chain
Earth - pottery, granite or crystal
Water - salted (ocean or pure water is best)
Wood - bowl, twigs, cork or a plant
Begin - light the candle...

Pour the salted water into the bowl, do not cover.

Play music.

Remove everything from the closet.

Put ALL items into four different priority piles.

- things you like/need and will keep
- items you need for later but not using
- things you love but are finished with – give away
- things to dispose

Throw away everything damaged, cracked or broken.

If you haven't used an item in the past 'six months', then it probably should be in the **'dispose'** pile. It is taking up the 'what-if' space and accumulating 'old' energies.

Have a bell to 'ring' to stir things up, shake up stale energies, especially in corners.

Do a thorough dusting and vacuuming of the space.

Wash down the walls.

Make any required repairs to the damaged areas.

If a stronger correction is required, then paint the space in an 'enhancing' color in latex paint.

All hangers should match in a closet and be the same type and color leaving 10% empty for new items.

Put back only things that are used, needed or loved, in an organized fashion.

Place items together in 'color' sections.

Nothing is to be on the floor... shoes on racks, in boxes or placed on shelves.

Always have empty hangers and open space (ready to accept 'new').

Add natural fragrance OR eucalyptus.

Light fixture must always be in good repair.

For Maximum Correction

It is vital to your health to consider the removal of all off-gassing plastics, synthetics, materials and products containing volatile chemicals. (Especially in children's rooms.)

> Everything should appear spacious,
> Not crowded or cramped.

List three areas in your home where **you** spend the majority of your time.

Example:
bedroom stay - 8 hours
kitchen time - 4 hours
home office work - 6 hours

Element Enhancement
The three areas that you have selected are the rooms you should apply enhancements and/or controls, new furniture realignment, color analysis, and accessorize after a complete space cleansing.

***

Results: following your cleanse, you will sense a new feeling of being...

Motivated
Clear-headed
Less burdened
Revitalized
Content
Balanced
Healthier
Rested and relaxed
Focused
Cheerful and upbeat
Positive attitude
Rested and sleep better
Independent
Self-confident
Behavioural changes
Removed energy blocks
Everything seems newer
A sense of well-being

Ready to conquer life's challenges, again.

You will achieve the best results by observing and developing the *'ability to survive and thrive with nature'* by removing negative energy, and by giving room for universal, positive energy.

Nature is a delicate balance of all elements constantly interacting with each other in a continuous cycle of creation.
"Go with the flow" and be in harmony with your environment.

***

(Nine)
WISDOM

All energy source comes from the power of the sun
which has accumulated in the earth:
light inhaled by plants,
buried in coal, mineral fields;
converts water into vapor, then to rain or snow,
which is released back into the earth.

No life of any kind can exist without 'sun' energy
as it is the source of life itself
animal, vegetable and mineral.

***

Be there,
where you are to be.
Speak,
when you are to speak.
Beware!
You are there... consciously.

***

Be in the 'moment'
Look around your environment
Yesterday is 'today past'
Tomorrow is 'today future'
They are all ' today now'
Do what You need to do.... now!

***

Look around your exterior, interior and 'inside thoughts'.
Don't bring your 'past' to the 'present'
Because it will dominate your 'future'.

***

The 'dragon energy' within
is an indication of coming to terms
with ones passions & chaotic beliefs
in order to become a custodian of one's own future.

***

Change is our ability to grow!
Burn off negative energy
with regular daily physical exercise.
Moderate your emotions for clarity.

***

The 'eye' of the construction; peak of the pyramid
is the element 'earth' centre.
This center area of a building or room should remain
clear of obstruction.

***

The cornerstone of a building
is the 'living heart' of its foundation.

***

A strong, well-fed, rested body
has a sharp memory and mind.

***

The flow & balance
of natural energies lies between
(FENG) wind on earth = the breath of the body within.
(SHUI) water on earth = the body of humans within.
A relationship with the environment is created
when this is harmonized and in balance.

***

Before you begin <u>any</u> activity,
always start by enhancing positive energy
in and around you with three very deep breaths.
Inhale into the stomach
making it expand; then tightening it as you exhale.
This will always bring your senses
into a clear awareness state.

***

Ancient cultures would cleanse
by placing the flat palms of their hands over ears firmly
then quickly release 10 times.

***

Fly a flag
stating your desires of giving and receiving
written on it - and fly this powerful affirmation.

***

Healing water
was considered that which has rested
in an Earth container (glass)
in the sun for 3 hours.
(Drink whenever and as much as possible)

***

Change comes to you when you become detached.
Be silent. Still the mind. Be a *'choiceless watcher'*
of your environment, who only hears and sees.
A new vibrant energy rises to the surface,
a new awareness.

***

Everyone sees you differently.
A neighbor, a gardener, a teacher,
a parent, a child, a complainer, an athlete.
All have very different personalities.
List 25 different identities you have had
since childhood, and then
contemplate these different energies
as either positive or negative.
The yin/yang usually
balance out.

***

Break routine.
Always walk, drive and travel a different way
to work to renew energy and
stimulate the visual.

***

An Observer's energy can actually
influence an experiment.

***

Earth's energy-flow changes each year.
All years ending in an *odd* number carry *Yin energy*
and *even* numbers carry *Yang energy.*

Years ending 0 or 1 carry *Metal* energy
Water energy is for years ending in 2 or 3.
Years ending in 4 or 5 carry *Wood* energy and
Fire energy exists in years ending in 6 and 7.
The flow of *Earth* energy is for years ending in 8 and 9.

***

You carry the energy of your birth year,
all the days of your life.
Babies born in 2007 carry Yin Fire energy
throughout their life.

***

Sha ch'i = bad Feng Shui
Too much or not enough = Negative energy
Water = storms, tsunami or drought
Wind = hurricanes, blizzards or stagnant, decay
Too many words = arguments or lack of communication
Not enough food or too much food = illness
Too much sleep or not enough sleep = poor health
Too much 'stuff' (clutter) or not enough 'needs' = anxiety
Too many shoes or not the right pair needed = frustration
No pencils or dozens of them... etc

***

Good ch'i = positive plus negative
'energy' in perfect balance.

***

You can't do tomorrow what you can do today
when your passion and energy are at their peak.
Time just passes you by.

NOTES:

(Ten)
Question & Answers

My family consists of my dog and me. I have moved to a new home and find that he is very restless and doesn't want to settle down.

Animals have strong instincts. He is obviously not comfortable as animals also have positive energy fields and when they find a room and can lie around for hours, you know they found it. My cat would lie on a small chair I had in the bathroom while the dog would lay anywhere he could find in the sun. He did not stay in one place too long, though. We are all happier when we find our best locations. Unless the home is carrying negative energy from some mishap that he senses, he will eventually settle.

***

Should I buy some tassels to activate the energy and put a turtle in the north for career enhancement?

Unless you were born with an Asian background, we don't have this following in our culture. Less is best to activate a change in energy... so that the energy can reach your desires. Place or write what you want to happen in your career (north) sector, with photos, books or written affirmations. The enhancements are black/white or metal and water items and nothing else. Pink light bulbs, tassels, dragons are not North American enhancements.

***

I'm in school still, and am having a terrible time with one of my subjects which I have to get to graduate.

The knowledge sector is the northeast area of a room, which is a good place to keep you texts. Keep your desk clear of other subjects. Pay attention to where you are actually studying this subject now. Are you sitting elsewhere or lying down? You could be in one of your negative spaces making it impossible to grasp it. You also need to do deep breathing before studying, as you must relax to absorb the knowledge. Also, chat with another student who does well in it. I recommend a large red candle when studying which sits in the northeast area. Also, place a crystal on top of the books you are studying.

***

I have a studio condo and need assistance on how to begin?

Take a compass and align it with the entry door to see what energy the condo carries. By looking *into* the unit, a northeast, west, southwest or northwest reading would be a *West sitting* condo, and south, north, east and southeast would be an *East sitting* condo. Does this match *your energy*, which you carry from your birth year?

Your energy charts will provide you with a Pa Kua number and your best location for your bed, desk/office, eating/dining etc. You use these locations to set up your home furnishings. What is your first impression when you enter? Does the space talk to you, feel good?

***

What is my first consideration before buying or renting?

Regardless of the décor, does the space *'feel'* good to you?
Is there good sunlight within the structure?
Can you live there for several years?
Is there adequate space for your lifestyle?
Be aware of what appears damaged or broken that needs fixing *before* you relocate.
How many sharp corners, overhead beams, hanging lights are there? What you are doing is looking for negative energy.

***

I love our new house, but my partner does not feel the same.

Your partner's inner intuition is warning him of something negative. You should investigate the previous owners and find out why they sold. Was there a financial problem or illness? There may be some bad energy left from the previous owners, but could easily be corrected with an interior realignment once it is specified. If it is not feeling good for him, he should try entering from another doorway, or renovate the problems. Check to see if there are missing areas due to the shape of the structure.

My new office building faces directly onto an oncoming road. I don't like this *feeling* that one day someone might crash into me.

Your intuition is correct. Any home or business suffers harsh and negative energy entering their premises in this type of situation. Some recommended corrections are:

- a curved or meandering walkway.

- a protective stone, or landscaped enclosure or fence.

- the entry door to be recessed and installed on an angle to divert this strong, incoming energy.

- plant tall, flowering shrubs/plants on each side of the door.

- a protective covering to the entry door or a solid wood door.

- an octagon shaped mirror placed (centred) above the main door reflecting this harsh energy.

***

My garden around my front entrance is a disaster as nothing we are planting grows in the north in this soil.

It is time to make changes to this area to attract positive energy by removing it all, totally. Nurture the soil for three weeks. Redesign the space with limited flowering shrubs and consider creating a container garden where you are in control. Plant numerous seasonal flowers, but all to be in one color, white. (This is a metal-energy color, which enhances the north sector of the home) Try to select round leaf shrubs and plants.

***

We have recently downsized and are now living in a town-bungalow and find it very dark because we are in the middle.

Living in a rowhouse situation needs special attention to brighten and enhance the atmosphere. Small spaces and dark areas need light or pastel walls mixed with light colored furniture that has contrasting piping, pillows, and drapery rods and dark framed artwork. Keep the floors a medium color tone that is between these two contrasts. This yin/yang color combination keeps the energy meandering and positive. A splash of red in the south, northeast or southwest works well in any space.

***

My sister drives me nuts with her dozens of shoes all over the place that she never puts away.

Shoes protect us from harmful matter and diseases. You just never know where they have walked along the way, and unless they're kept under control, on shelves, mats or in boxes, the energy they have picked up resonates throughout the space. This shoe-clutter can create anxiety, arguments, even laziness as well as anger when not being used. You can only wear one pair at a time, so the rest should be organized, cared for and put in a special place created for them, out of sight. No need for unnecessary havoc.

***

My job keeps me busy, and I am having difficulty with the constant pick-up of kid's toys all the time.

Children like to copy others. If they see a tidy, organized room, and shown that they have a special place for their things that is strictly theirs; they tend to learn at a young age. Your environment is a reflection of how others treat you. Consider chairs or footstools that can be used or opened for their own storage.

***

I live in the tiniest place on this planet. I cannot even find a place for the ironing board, which I use almost every day.

An iron is Fire-energy and *not* meant to be left out in the open. Be creative, make a funky cover for the ironing board, and hang it on the wall, like a surfboard or unique photo board. It will then turn into something loved and the negative energy will turn positive. We all have things we use daily, but make sure of organization and do not show *unfinished work,* which could just be laziness. Consider options and be creative with storage spaces. Good fun schway!

***

Change the energy and you can change your life!

**Enjoy more books
by Author
Mallory Neeve Wilkins**

Non-Fiction
Ancient Secrets for a Healthy Home (ebook & hardcover)

Fiction
House of the Caduceus (ebook & paperback) Mystery-spiritual novel
Hot-Walker Life on the Fast Track (ebook & paperback) Sports Crime Romance Novel

Photography
The Laundry Art Book
Graveyard Autos

www.ingramcontent.com/pod-product-compliance
Lightning Source LLC
Chambersburg PA
CBHW050646160426
43194CB00010B/1834